D0098145

The Canadian
HERITAGE
CHRISTMAS
Cookbook

The Canadian HERITAGE CHRISTMAS *Cookbook*

Edna McCann

Prentice Hall Canada Inc.
Scarborough, Ontario

Canadian Cataloguing in Publication Data

McCann, Edna
       The Canadian heritage Christmas cookbook

ISBN 0-13-897596-5

1. Christmas cookery. 2. Cookery, Canadian. I. Title.

TX739.2.C45M32 1997   641.5'68   C97-931988-9

 © 1998 Prentice-Hall Canada Inc., Scarborough, Ontario
A Division of Simon & Schuster/A Viacom Company

Prentice-Hall, Inc., Upper Saddle River, New Jersey
Prentice-Hall International (UK) Limited, London
Prentice-Hall of Australia, Pty. Limited, Sydney
Prentice-Hall Hispanoamericana, S.A., Mexico City
Prentice-Hall of India Private Limited, New Delhi
Prentice-Hall of Japan, Inc., Tokyo
Simon & Schuster Southeast Asia Private Limited, Singapore
Editora Prentice-Hall do Brasil, Ltda., Rio de Janeiro

ISBN 0-13-897596-5

Acquisitions Editor: Jill Lambert
Managing Editor: Robert Harris
Copy Editor: Ruth Pincoe
Production Editor: Mary Ann McCutcheon
Production Coordinator: Julie Preston

Photo Research: Susan Wallace-Cox
Cover and Interior Design: Julia Hall
Cover Image: Larry Williams/Masterfile
Page Layout: B.J. Weckerle

1 2 3 4 5   F   02 01 00 99 98

Printed and bound in Canada

Visit the Prentice Hall Canada Web site! Send us your comments, browse our catalogues, and more. **www.phcanada.com**

Photo Credits – Page 3, Glenbow Museum; **page 15**, Glenbow Museum/NA-2968-40; **page 27**, Corbis-Bettmann; **page 39**, Mike Filey Collection; **page 51**, UPI/Corbis-Bettmann; **page 63**, Mike Filey Collection; **page 75**, Corbis-Bettmann; **page 87**, Glenbow Museum/NA-1128-1; **page 99**, Corbis-Bettmann; **page 111**, Glenbow Museum/NA-2436-13; **page 123**, UPI/Corbis-Bettmann; **page 135**, Corbis-Bettmann

Table of Contents

For many of us of the Christian faith, no holiday, throughout the year, is anticipated with more joy and delight than Christmas. There is a wealth of customs and traditions associated with the Christmas season, but above all it is a time to appreciate the love of family and friends. It is a time of giving and receiving, a time of inspiration and hope, of peace on earth, good will to men.

Two things are usually true about the holiday season. First, no matter how early you begin preparations, you always have last minute things to do and you feel that there is never enough time. Second, the time and effort that you put into buying gifts, trimming the tree, and all the other activities associated with this time of celebration are worth every minute because these are what precious memories are made of.

THE FOURTH SUNDAY BEFORE Christmas marks the beginning of Advent. For most families, this is the beginning of the Christmas season.

In our family, the season actually began the Sunday before Advent, on "Stir-Up" Sunday. This was the day set aside for making the mincemeat and the Christmas puddings and cake. The name "stir-up" comes from the collect for that day in the Anglican *Book of Common Prayer*: "Stir-up, we beseech thee, O Lord, the wills of thy faithful people; that they, plenteously bringing forth the fruit of good works, may of thee be plenteously rewarded; through Jesus Christ our Lord."

On this weekend, as these foods are being prepared, every person who came into the house would stir each pot three times, once each in the name of the Father, the Son and the Holy Ghost. It was a quaint old practice with practical home pleasures. I taught my children to keep Stir-Up weekend and they have passed the tradition on to their children as well.

Although this recipe for Christmas fruit cake may be just a little different from what you are used to, it is really delicious!

Christmas Fruit Cake

2 cups dried pears

4 cups water

1 cup dried apricots

2 cups water

3 cups whole wheat pastry flour

1/2 tsp salt

1/4 cup soya oil

1 cup walnuts, roasted and chopped

1 tsp vanilla extract

Rind of 1 orange

Orange juice

Preheat the oven to 350°F and oil a 9 × 5-inch loaf pan.

Place pears in 4 cups water in a saucepan. Cover, simmer for 30 minutes, then purée. Place apricots and 2 cups water in a saucepan. Cover, simmer for 30 minutes, then chop.

Merry Christmas

4701

Combine flour and salt. Mix the oil into the flour by hand.

Add the pear purée, chopped apricots, walnuts, vanilla and orange rind to the flour mixture and mix in enough orange juice to make a moist batter. Pour into an oiled pan and bake for 2–2 1/2 hours.

The cake will keep well in the refrigerator, or the freezer. Wrap in foil or plastic wrap.

MY CHILDREN WERE NOT great fans of that old Christmas favourite, mincemeat, but they loved mother's mincemeat oatmeal cookies. I hope that your family will enjoy them as well.

Mincemeat Oatmeal Cookies

1/2 cup softened shortening

1 cup light brown sugar, firmly packed

1 egg

1 1/2 cups prepared mincemeat

1 1/2 cups all-purpose flour, sifted

3/4 tsp baking soda

1/2 tsp salt

1 1/2 cups quick cooking oats

Preheat the oven to 375°F and grease a cookie sheet.

Cream shortening and sugar together well, then beat in the egg. Add the mincemeat, mixing thoroughly.

Sift the flour with baking soda and salt and add to the mincemeat mixture. Stir in the oatmeal, mixing well. Drop by tablespoonfuls onto a greased cookie sheet.

Bake for about 15 minutes. Cool on a wire rack.

Yield: about 3 1/2 dozen.

NO CHRISTMAS DINNER IN our home was complete without steamed plum pudding and hard sauce. Although we most often made our plum pudding in a large mold, small plum puddings make attractive gifts. When thoroughly cooled, wrap them first in plastic and then in attractive gift paper.

Plum Pudding

1 cup soft bread crumbs

1 cup seedless raisins

1 cup currants

1 cup chopped dates

1/2 cup chopped citron peel

1/2 cup chopped walnuts

1 cup all-purpose flour

1 tsp baking powder

1/4 tsp baking soda

1/4 tsp salt

1/2 tsp cinnamon

1/4 tsp ground nutmeg

1/4 tsp ground cloves

1/4 tsp ground allspice

1/2 cup butter

1/2 cup brown sugar

2 eggs

1/3 cup molasses

1 cup milk

Combine the bread crumbs, fruit and nuts with a small amount of flour. Stir the flour, baking powder, baking soda, salt and spices together.

In a large bowl, cream the butter and sugar together well. Add the eggs one at a time, beating well after each. Blend in molasses. Add milk alternatively with the flour mixture, beginning and ending with flour. Fold in the fruit, nuts and bread crumbs.

Pour batter into a greased 1 1/2-quart pudding bowl or small individual molds filling about 2/3 full, and cover tightly.

Steam about 3 hours for large mold or 1–2 hours for small molds.

Serve hot with sauce.

A lovely way to serve plum pudding is as a wreath. Steam the pudding in a ring mold, and turn it out on a serving dish decorated with holly leaves or small pine branches. Add red and green cherries or candied citron to complete the Christmas wreath.

Hard Sauce for Plum Pudding

1/2 cup butter

3/4 cup brown sugar

3/4 cup icing sugar

1/3 cup whipping cream

1 tsp vanilla

2 tsp. brandy (optional)

Cream the butter and gradually add the sugars, beating thoroughly. Slowly add cream and vanilla, beating constantly. Pile the sauce into a dish. Make a well in the centre, add the brandy, and let sit until brandy is soaked up. Chill before serving. Serve with hot plum pudding.

Yield: 1 1/2 cups

> *"Now is the season of the holly and the mistletoe;*
> *the days are come in which we hang our rooms*
> *with the sober green of December*
> *and feel it summer in our hearts."*

Saturday Evening Post
December 29, 1866

DURING THE FOUR WEEKS of Advent, the first period of preparation for Christ's coming, we celebrate with services and devotions at church and in our home. There are a number of Advent traditions that have come from Europe to North America.

The circular shape of an Advent wreath symbolizes God's eternal love and the candles symbolize Christ as the light of the world. The traditional wreath has five candles; four are purple, denoting royalty, and one—the Christ candle, which is lit December 24—is white, signifying purity. In Europe, Advent wreaths were suspended from the ceiling and the candles were lit one by one on each of the four Sundays before Christmas. The Advent wreath, brought to North America by early settlers, is still popular but is usually laid flat, on a table or on a mantle.

THE ADVENT CALENDAR, a German custom, may take many forms. Sometimes it is a picture of a Christmas scene with numbered windows; one is opened each day to reveal a smaller Christmas scene or a line of scripture. A more popular children's calendar has a delicious piece of chocolate hidden behind each window. When I was a girl, my mother made a calendar for each of us. We opened our chocolate window each morning just after breakfast.

The first day of Advent was always a cause for celebration and an excuse to enjoy a special meal. We didn't have a set favourite menu; instead, each person in the family was given a chance to pick something that they particularly wanted. This sometimes led to a rather strange and unique combination of foods, but to us kids, it made the dinner all the more special.

Here are a few of our family's favourite recipes for Advent dinner.

Butternut Squash Soup with Cinnamon Croutons

For the soup:

1 small leek

1 1/2 tbsp margarine or butter

1 medium carrot, coarsely chopped

1 small onion, coarsely chopped

1 butternut squash (1–1 1/2 pounds) peeled and cut into
*   1-inch cubes*

1 cup chicken broth

1/4 tsp salt

1/4 cup light cream

For the croutons:

2 cups French bread, cut in 3/4-inch cubes

1 1/2 tsp margarine or butter, melted

1/8 tsp ground cinnamon

Dash of salt

To prepare croutons: preheat oven to 400°F. In a bowl, toss the bread cubes with the margarine, ground cinnamon and salt. Spread the bread cubes on a baking sheet and bake 8 to 10 minutes or until golden brown.

Cut off the root of the leek. Cut the leek lengthwise in half and rinse with cold running water to remove sand. Coarsely chop the white and pale green part of the leek. Discard the dark green part.

In a large saucepan or Dutch oven, melt margarine over medium heat. Add carrots, onion and leek and cook 10 minutes, stirring occasionally. Add squash, chicken broth, salt and 1 cup water. Heat to boiling then reduce heat to low; cover and simmer 15 to 20 minutes or until the squash is tender.

Spoon a third of the squash mixture into a blender; cover and blend until smooth. Pour purée into a bowl. Repeat until all of the squash mixture is puréed. Return squash mixture to saucepan.

Just before serving, stir in the cream and heat the soup until hot but not boiling, stirring occasionally. Serve with cinnamon croutons.

Serves 6

Chicken Legs with Lemon, Garlic, and Rosemary

6 whole chicken legs

3 lemons, halved

3 tsp dried rosemary, crumbled

3 tbsp olive oil

3 cloves garlic, minced

1/3 cup water

Salt and pepper to taste

Pat the chicken dry and rub all over with the lemon halves (use 1/2 lemon for two legs). Season with salt, pepper and half of the rosemary.

In a large heavy skillet heat the olive oil until hot but not smoking and sauté the chicken, skin side down, for 7 to 8 minutes or until golden brown. Turn chicken, drizzle with the juice from the remaining lemon halves, and cook, covered, over moderately low heat about 1/2 hour or until cooked through.

Transfer chicken to a serving plate. Add the garlic and the remaining rosemary to the skillet and sauté over moderately high heat until just golden. Add water, scraping to loosen brown bits and simmer 1 minute. Drizzle sauce over the chicken. Serve with oven-roasted potatoes.

Serves 6

THE MEMBERS OF OUR family take desserts seriously. When we were young, the rule was that our dinner plate had to be clean before we were allowed to help ourselves to dessert. This was particularly tough for my brother Ben as he was quite a finicky eater and particularly despised vegetables. Mother felt that it was her duty to make the dessert delicious in direct proportion to Ben's dislike of a main-course dish. It was a challenge. "If I make a chocolate chiffon pie, I wonder if I can get Ben to eat asparagus." Likewise, Ben would often try to bargain: "If I eat four spoons of squash, would you make apple crisp for dessert?"

This tradition has carried through the generations. My great-grandson Justin considers ketchup and relish on a hot dog to be a complete serving of vegetables because "It's tomatoes and cucumbers, Gran."

On the McCann scale of dessert equivalents, this next recipe is worth one serving each of turnip and beets and three Brussels spouts.

Chocolate Box Cake with Berries and Cream

6 ounces semisweet chocolate

1 tbsp shortening

6 ounces cream cheese, softened

4 tbsp butter (not margarine), softened

1 1/2 cups confectioners' sugar

1/3 cup unsweetened cocoa

2 tbsp milk

1 tsp vanilla extract

2 cups whipping cream

2 pints strawberries

Mint leaves for garnish

Start this dish early in the day to allow time for chilling.

Line a 9 × 9-inch baking pan as smoothly as possible with aluminum foil.

In a small heavy saucepan over low heat, melt chocolate and shortening, stirring frequently. Pour the melted chocolate into the foil-lined pan and swirl it around the sides so that the entire inside of the pan is covered. Refrigerate for 1 minute then swirl the chocolate a second time to reinforce the sides of the chocolate box. Refrigerate until the chocolate is firm (about 30 minutes).

In a large bowl, with mixer at medium speed, beat cream cheese and butter until smooth. Add sugar, cocoa, milk and vanilla, and beat until fluffy. In a small bowl, beat 1 1/2 cups of whipping cream until stiff, and fold it into the cream cheese mixture.

Remove the foil-lined chocolate box from the pan and carefully peel off the foil. Place the chocolate box on a serving platter and fill with the cream cheese mixture. Refrigerate until the filling is firm (about 2 hours).

In a small bowl, beat the remaining 1/2 cup of whipping cream until stiff peaks form. Spoon into a decorating bag and pipe a 1-inch border around the edges of the box. Arrange strawberry halves over the top of the filling. Garnish with mint leaves. Slice the remaining berries to serve separately.

O come, O come, Emmanuel,
And ransom captive Israel
That mourns in lowly exile here
Until the Son of God appear.
Rejoice! Rejoice! Emmanuel
Shall come to thee, O Israel.

9th-century Latin antiphon translated
by John Mason Neale

CHRISTMAS CARDS ARE A favourite way to send good wishes during the holiday season.

For centuries, letters of Christmas news, blessings and good cheer were dispatched to faraway friends and isolated family members or clergy. Early in the nineteenth century, British art students made detailed scrolls of Christmas greetings with artwork and calligraphy.

During the 1840s, a printer employed by Queen Victoria sent cards with Christmas greetings to many of his friends. The idea caught the attention of the Queen, and her husband Prince Albert. John Calcott Horsley, a member of the Royal Academy and a respected illustrator of the day, was commissioned by H.R.H. to design a Christmas card. It was lithographed, hand tinted, and in 1846 sold a thousand copies at a shilling apiece.

Today Christmas cards are a multi-million-dollar business as people around the world send greetings to friends and relatives.

My daughter Marg and I usually set aside several days in late November or early December to do our cards. As I like to add a personal note or letter in each, it often takes many hours of writing before I am ready to send them on their way. To save time and energy on card preparation days, it is a good idea to plan some dishes that are easily made or can be prepared in advance and re-heated to serve.

Hot soups are some of my favourite dishes. The following recipes make a warm and satisfying quick-fix lunch or dinner.

Cream of Mushroom Soup

3/4 lb fresh mushrooms

3 tbsp plus 4 tbsp butter

1 1/4 quarts chicken broth or consommé

1/2 cup chopped onion

1/4 cup flour

1/2 cup heavy cream

1/2 tsp salt

1/4 tsp freshly ground white pepper

1 tbsp Worcestershire sauce

1/4 cup sherry

Wash the mushrooms, pat dry, and cut into 1/8-inch slices. (Do not remove the stems.)

Melt 3 tbsp butter in a medium stockpot or saucepan, add the mushrooms and sauté for about 5 minutes, turning frequently so that all are exposed equally to the heat.

Add chicken broth to the pot, then add the chopped onions. Cover and simmer over medium heat for about 30 minutes, until the onions are tender.

Strain the soup, reserving the liquid, and transfer the vegetables to a food mill (or a coarse sieve). Pass the vegetables through the mill (or push them through the sieve with a wooden spoon) and combine with the broth in the stockpot (off the heat).

In a small saucepan, melt the remaining butter (do not allow it to brown). Stir in the flour to make a paste and cook for about 2 minutes, stirring frequently. Add the cream, a little at a time, to make a smooth heavy cream sauce. Stir the cream sauce into the soup and add the salt, pepper, Worcestershire sauce and sherry.

Warm the soup slowly over low heat (do not allow it to boil) and keep hot until serving time.

HINT: The chance of scorching cream soup is much reduced if you heat the soup, after the cream has been added, in a double boiler. Frequent stirring will also help prevent scorching.

Vegetable Barley Soup

1 good sized soup marrow bone (2–3 pounds), cracked
1 pound chuck beef, cubed
2 tbsp butter
2 1/2 quarts water
1 1/2 tsp salt
1/4 tsp pepper
1 1/2 tsp sugar
2 tbsp minced fresh parsley
(or 1 tbsp dried)
1/4 cup barley
1 cup diced carrots
2 cups cooked tomatoes (skins off)
1/4 cup finely chopped onions
1/2 cup finely chopped celery
1 cup peas

1 cup cubed potatoes

1/2 cup chopped cabbage

Put soup bone in a large pot. In another pan, brown the beef lightly in the butter and add to the large pot. Add water, salt, pepper, sugar, and parsley. Bring to a boil, cover and simmer for 1 hour. Skim the surface occasionally. Add barley and simmer 1 hour longer. Add carrots, tomatoes, onions and celery. Cover and simmer 45 minutes. Add remaining ingredients and simmer 15 minutes more.

Serves 6 to 8

Although squash is not always a favourite vegetable, even the teenagers in our family like this squash and carrot soup.

Cream of Squash and Carrot Soup

1 medium onion, diced

2 tbsp salad oil

2 acorn squashes (about 1 1/4 pounds each)

4 carrots (about 3/4 pounds)

1 14-ounce can chicken broth

3/4 tsp salt

1/4 tsp pepper

1 cup half and half cream

2 tsp chopped fresh dill or 1/4 tsp dried dill

2 1/2 cups water

Dill sprigs for garnish

Heat 1 tablespoon of salad oil in a 4-quart saucepan. Add the onion and cook over medium heat until tender (about 15 minutes). Remove the onion to a plate.

Cut each squash in half. Scoop out and discard the seeds. Peel the squash and carrots and cut into 1-inch chunks. Heat 1 tablespoon of salad oil in the same saucepan. Add the squash and carrot and cook over medium heat until golden brown, stirring occasionally.

Return onion to the saucepan. Stir in the chicken broth, salt, pepper and water. Heat to boiling, then reduce heat to low. Cover and simmer until squash and carrot are tender (about 30 minutes), stirring frequently.

Spoon a third of the squash mixture into a blender; cover and blend until smooth. Pour purée into a bowl. Repeat until all of the squash mixture is puréed.

Return soup to saucepan and stir in the dill and cream. Cook over medium heat, stirring occasionally, until the soup is heated through.

Garnish with dill springs and serve with crusty French or Italian bread.

Serves 8 as a first course

The very name of Christmas
Has sparkle in its sound.
It has the shine of tinsel,
Of crisp and frosty ground.

It prickles with a fragrance
Of spicy northern pine
Whose fresh and pungent perfume
Is part of Christmastime.

YEARS AGO, WHEN WE decorated our home, the time I loved the most was when Ben, Sarah, Dad and I would go to the woods to get pine boughs for the Advent wreaths. We also used pine boughs to decorate the mantle and to wrap around the banister and newel post as a garland. Mother would make popcorn and hot drinks to warm us when we arrived home. To this day, the smell of pine brings back the memories of these joyful occasions.

A hot drink is a nice way to warm up after a chilly outing in the woods. A cinnamon stick added to a cup of hot chocolate gives this old favourite a different taste.

Hot Chocolate with Cinnamon Sticks

8 tbsp Dutch or Swiss cocoa powder

8 tbsp of sugar

2 cups of milk

1/2 cup boiling water

1 tsp nutmeg

4 cinnamon sticks

In a saucepan, mix together the sugar and cocoa. Add the boiling water and stir with a wooden spoon until the powder and sugar dissolve into a thick syrup. (Heat gently if necessary to dissolve all of the contents.) Stir in milk and warm over medium heat until just short of boiling. Stir in the nutmeg.

Serve in mugs with a cinnamon stick as a garnish.

Serves 4

My son-in-law Bruce enjoys a hot toddy once or twice in a winter. This recipe comes from his grandfather.

Hot Toddy

6 eggs

8 tsp granulated sugar

1/2 cup rum

1/2 cup brandy

3 cups boiling water

Grated nutmeg for garnish

Combine eggs and sugar and beat well. Add the rum and brandy and carefully stir in the boiling water. Serve hot in earthenware mugs with nutmeg sprinkled on top.

Serves 6

Hot buttered milk was one of my mother's favourites. She often made this treat when we came in from skating or tobogganing.

Hot Buttered Milk

1 quart milk

1/3 cup light brown sugar, firmly packed

4 tbsp butter or margarine

Grated nutmeg for garnish

Combine milk, brown sugar and butter in a medium saucepan. Heat slowly, stirring constantly until butter melts. (Do not let the milk boil.) Pour into mugs and sprinkle with nutmeg.

Serves 4 to 6

SOMETHING THAT WE ALL enjoy at this time of year is the traditional eggnog. The commercial eggnog you can buy these days is good, but I really think the best eggnog I have tasted is that which my mother made from our old family recipe. It is not difficult to make and I think you'll agree that it is delicious and worth the effort.

Eggnog

6 eggs, separated

1/2 to 3/4 cup sugar

2 cups milk

3 cups heavy cream

2 tsp vanilla extract or rum extract

Grated nutmeg for garnish

In a large bowl, beat the egg whites until stiff but not dry, gradually adding the sugar. In another bowl, beat the yolks until they are lemon yellow. Fold the egg whites into the egg yolks.

In a third bowl, beat the cream until stiff. Add it to the egg mixture along with the milk and vanilla, stirring gently. Chill well. Sprinkle with grated nutmeg just before serving. (The eggnog may need to be stirred gently before serving.)

Serves 8

THIS INTERESTING VARIATION OF my mother's recipe adds the flavour of pumpkin, another Christmas favourite in our home.

Pumpkin Eggnog

2 eggs, separated

1/2 cup sugar

1/2 cup pumpkin purée

4 cups half and half cream

1/4 cup Jamaican rum

Pumpkin spice for garnish

In a large bowl, beat the egg whites until stiff but not dry, gradually adding sugar. In another bowl, beat the egg yolks until they are lemon yellow. Beat the pumpkin purée into the egg yolks, then fold in the egg whites.

In a third bowl, beat the cream until it is frothy. Add to the egg mixture along with the rum. Stir to blend and chill.

Serve very cold. Sprinkle with a dash of pumpkin spice before serving. (If the eggnog is served to adults, some hosts prefer to increase the rum to 2 cups.)

Serves 6

EARLY IN DECEMBER IS A good time to think about gifts from the kitchen. A homemade gourmet gift provides a special personal touch that you cannot buy, even in the most exclusive shops. As well, any present that you make yourself is a special compliment, since so few people have the time to make their own jams, jellies, cookies, cakes or candies.

One of the most popular Christmas gifts, which has become quite a tradition in our family, is homemade jam. Each summer, at the height of the fruit season, I prepare jars of preserves and jellies. In December, I cover the tops with Christmas material and decorate the jars with festive red and green bows.

They are always a welcome gift. As my husband George used to say, "You can never have too much homemade jam." One of his favourite breakfasts was whole grain toast smothered with strawberry preserves. My dear friend Eleanor provided me with this new recipe for Strawberry Banana Jam, and I am sure that George would have approved.

Strawberry-Banana Jam

4 3/4 cups prepared fruit (about 2 quarts of fully ripened strawberries and 3 fully ripened bananas)

3 tbsp fresh lemon juice

6 3/4 cups sugar

1 box fruit pectin

1/2 tsp margarine or butter

To sterilize the jars, cover them with water and boil for 15 minutes. Keep them hot in the sterilizing water until you fill them. (Do not boil self-sealing lids as it hurts their ability to seal.)

Stem and crush strawberries, one layer at a time. Measure out 3 1/4 cups and place in a large saucepan. Mash the bananas thoroughly. Measure out 1 1/2 cups and add to the saucepan. Stir in the lemon juice and fruit pectin and add the margarine.

Bring mixture to a boil and boil for exactly one minute, stirring constantly. Remove from heat and skim away any foam from the top. Ladle into hot sterilized jars, filling to 1/8 inch from the top.

Wipe jar rims and threads. Cover with two-piece lids, screwing the bands tightly. Invert jars for 5 minutes, then turn upright. Check the seals after the jars are cool.

Makes 8 1-cup jars

AS I MENTIONED EARLIER, small plum puddings make excellent gifts. In Victorian times, it was the custom to wrap silver charms in a bit of paper and hide them in the Christmas pudding. Mothers were usually able to slice the pudding so that each child received a charm. Each charm had a name: Bell of Betrothal, Thimble of Blessedness, Wishbone, Coin of Fortune, Bachelor's Button and Horseshoe of Luck.

Whenever Marg and I make plum puddings to give as gifts, we wrap coins in paper and hide them in the puddings. (Warn the recipient that you have done this so as to prevent a broken tooth at Christmas dinner.)

You can wrap the puddings in plastic and festive paper. Another option is to pack them in decorative, air-tight metal tins to add a special touch to your gift.

Chocolate truffles, presented in a simple box lined with gold foil and trimmed with Christmas ribbon, make a luxury gift that all will welcome.

There are many different recipes for chocolate truffles. I prefer one that comes from my dear friend Peggy, who lives in the Cotswold Hills in southwest England. These truffles make a truly elegant gift that chocolate lovers will rave about for months.

Chocolate Truffles

5 tbsp heavy cream or whipping cream

*8 ounces (plus 12 ounces, optional) milk chocolate, broken
    into small pieces*

1–2 tbsp cognac (optional)

4 tbsp cocoa powder (for dusting)

Pour the cream into a small saucepan and heat gently until tepid. Put 8 ounces of chocolate pieces into a small bowl and melt gently over hot but not boiling water, stirring occasionally. (Do not let the bottom of the bowl sit in the hot water: it is essential that the chocolate does not overheat.)

When the chocolate has melted, remove the bowl from the heat. Slowly pour in the cream, in a gentle trickle, stirring thoroughly to mix.

Let the mixture cool a little and add the cognac (if using). Using a hand whisk or an electric beater on low speed, beat

until the mixture becomes lighter in colour and stands in peaks (usually 3 to 4 minutes). Refrigerate for about 20 minutes or until stiff.

Sprinkle the cocoa powder through the sieve onto a cookie sheet. Remove spoonfuls of the chocolate paste and roll into balls about 1 inch in diameter. Drop each ball into the cocoa powder and roll to cover. Leave the balls in a cool place until firm.

To cover the balls in chocolate, melt the remaining 12 ounces of chocolate over water as before. Using a thin wooden skewer, spear each ball and dip it into the melted chocolate, making sure that it is well covered. Place on tinfoil to set.

Makes 16 truffles

FOR MANY YEARS, I have collected small bottles and jars, and at Christmas time, I use them to make herb oils, which have become extremely popular. You can also purchase interesting jars and bottles at shops that sell collectibles or antiques.

Large grocery stores across Canada stock fresh herbs all year round. You can use almost any herb, but I have had the best success with basil, dill, rosemary and thyme.

Rinse the herbs under running water. Gently shake off the excess water and lay to dry on paper towels.

Make sure that the jars or bottles have been carefully washed; sterilization is not necessary.

Put the herbs into jars or bottles, fill with olive oil or sunflower oil, and seal thoroughly. Leave for at least two weeks before using.

Add a colourful bow for decoration and you have a simple but attractive gift.

IT SEEMS MANY PEOPLE are interested in healthy eating these days—low fat, low cholesterol, low sodium, the list grows longer every year. My daughter Marg has been trying out many of the new low-fat recipes, and she tells me they are much improved from the old "no fat, no taste" versions that I remember. Recently, Mary and Marg spent an afternoon baking some of Marg's homemade bread I love so much. I was delighted to try it out, and shocked to hear that it was a new recipe with very little fat and almost no cholesterol. It tasted divine! Here are a few of Mary's latest low-fat yet tasty recipes. These baked goods are also great Christmas giveaways, particularly for friends who are on restricted diets.

These three recipes call for Lighter Bake, a new alternative to shortening. Apple butter can also be substituted for shortening.

Yummy Low-Fat Banana Bread

2 egg whites
1 tbsp oil
1 tbsp Lighter Bake or apple butter

1/3 cup skim or 1% milk

1/2 cup granulated sugar

1/4 cup brown sugar

1 tsp salt

1 tsp baking soda

1 tsp baking powder

1 tsp vanilla extract

1 tsp cinnamon

3 medium to large ripe bananas

1 1/2 cups flour (whole wheat or all-purpose)

1/2 package semi-sweet chocolate chips (optional, but adds
*   a bit of zip)*

Preheat the oven to 350°F and spray a loaf pan with Pam (or grease it lightly).

Combine all ingredients except for bananas, flour and chocolate chips in a bowl. In a separate bowl, mash the bananas well with a fork and blend in the flour.

Mix together the contents of both bowls, stirring with a fork. Stir in chocolate chips, if using. Pour the batter into a loaf pan and sprinkle the top with a dash of cinnamon and sugar. Bake for 45 min, or until a knife comes out clean.

Cool and enjoy!

MY SON-IN-LAW BRUCE loves cookies and he says that these chocolate chip cookies are delicious even if they are low-fat.

Low-Fat Chewy Chocolate Chippers

1 cup packed brown sugar

1/2 cup white sugar

1/2 cup Lighter Bake or apple butter

1 egg

1 tsp vanilla

1 1/4 cups flour

1 tsp baking powder

1/2 tsp baking soda

1/2 tsp salt

2 cups (12 ounces) chocolate chips

Preheat the oven to 375°F and spray a cookie sheet with Pam (or grease it lightly).

Beat together the sugars, Lighter Bake, egg and vanilla in one bowl. In another bowl, combine the flour, baking soda and salt. Combine contents of both bowls, and stir in chocolate chips.

Drop in balls onto cookie sheet. Bake 8–9 minutes, or until golden brown.

Makes 3 1/2 to 4 dozen

MUFFIN LOVERS WILL ENJOY these apple muffins. They are delicious with a cup of tea at breakfast, and I find they also make a good snack in the afternoon. Children will love one of these muffins as an after-school or bedtime snack.

Low-Fat Fresh Apple Muffins

3/4 cup granulated sugar

1/3 cup Lighter Bake or apple butter

1 egg plus 1 egg white

1 1/2 tsp vanilla extract

2 1/2 cups peeled and diced tart green apples

1 1/2 cups flour

1 1/2 tsp baking soda

1 1/2 tsp cinnamon

1/2 tsp salt

3/4 cup raisins

Preheat oven to 350°F and spray regular muffin pan with Pam (or grease lightly).

Combine sugar, Lighter Bake, egg, egg white and vanilla in one bowl. Stir in the apples. In another bowl, combine the flour, baking soda, cinnamon, and salt.

Combine the contents of the two bowls, and stir in raisins. Spoon the batter into pans and add struesel topping if desired (see below). Bake 25 minutes or until knife comes out clean.

Yield: 12 muffins

Optional Struesel Topping:

1/4 cup sugar

2 tbsp flour

1/2 tsp cinnamon

2 tsp Lighter Bake or apple butter

Combine all ingredients to make fine crumb mix. Sprinkle on muffins before baking.

THIS NEXT DELECTABLE GIFT needs to be started in the summer, as different fresh fruits become available. Brandied Fruit can be used to make any number of desserts special, and it is delicious all year round. Our family enjoys it so much that we often run out around the Christmas season—you may want to make more than one batch at a time.

Brandied Fruit

This recipe begins with fine Cognac, the best that your budget will allow. You will also need a big old-fashioned stoneware crock with a heavy lid. A three-quart crock is probably about the right size. Collectable or antique stores will probably have large crocks in stock, or be able to find you one. When not being used to store fruit, these crocks make decorative indoor planters.

1 quart fine Cognac (or best possible brandy)

Grated rind of one orange

Grated rind of one lemon

Grated rind of one lime

12 whole cloves

6 whole allspice

1 quart ripe strawberries

3 cups sugar

Sweet cherries, stemmed

Ripe peaches, peeled, quartered and diced

Blackberries

Raspberries

Grapes

Sugar

Wash and rinse the crock thoroughly. Allow inside to dry completely. Pour in the cognac and add the grated rinds, whole spices, strawberries and sugar. Place a plate directly over the berries to hold them down in the Cognac. Cover the crock tightly and leave in a cool place for one week.

Add cherries, peaches, pineapple, blackberries, raspberries and grapes as they come into season. With each addition of fruit, add an equal amount of sugar. (I said this recipe was delicious, not low in calories!) Keep all the fruit submerged in the cognac by weighing it down with the plate. When all the fruit has been added, cover the crock tightly and let it stand in a cool place for three months.

To give as a gift, pack portions in clean jars, seal, and add a decorative bow. To keep for your own use, store the crock in a cool place.

MY GRANDSON MARSHALL AND his wife Jamie love peaches. Jamie's mom makes these Caramel Peaches. They are stored in jars and can be given as gifts. In our family we love to serve them with vanilla ice cream. Use crystal glasses and add a sprig of holly for a dessert that will impress at any festive dinner.

Caramel Peaches

4–5 pounds medium ripe peaches (enough to make 8 cups when peeled and sliced)
1/3 cup Cognac or good brandy
1 cup light brown sugar
4 cups granulated sugar

Peel and pit the peaches and slice about 1/4-inch thick—do not slice too thin. Combine peaches, Cognac and sugars in a preserving kettle. Bring slowly to a boil, stirring constantly until the sugar is dissolved, and simmer, stirring frequently, until the peaches are translucent and the syrup is thick.

Remove from heat and ladle immediately into clean sterilized jars that are still hot. Fill each jar to within 1/4 inch of the top and seal.

Makes 6–7 half-pint jars

Jamie added her own amusing story to the caramel peaches. One day Jamie and her mother were making up several large batches of caramel peaches. They had filled about a dozen jars and were preparing peaches for the next batch. When they turned around to look, they saw Michael, Jamie's two-year-old son, sitting on the kitchen table spooning peaches and brandy sauce into his little mouth as fast as he could. He and the table were covered in caramel peaches from head to toe. Neither Jamie nor her mother could keep a straight face as they chastised him.

THE CUSTOM OF DECORATING homes with evergreens and candles for winter festivals predates Christmas. The Romans decorated their villas to celebrate Saturnalia, the winter feast. The evergreen was a symbol of eternal life because it was able to survive the winter. Candles have been lighting holy days since the beginning of recorded time and today Christmas candles symbolize Christ, the Light of the World.

European tribes often hung evergreen circles on their doors to welcome friends and strangers to their homes. The circle was said to represent the continuous cycle of life. The Anglo-Saxons believed that mistletoe would protect houses against witchcraft and ensure fertility of those in the home. The Christmas wreath, traditionally made from evergreen branches, is thought to have originated as a symbol of Christ's crown of thorns.

Wreaths are as popular today as they were in Victorian times, although many people choose to use the artificial wreaths. The evergreens and berries on these mass-produced wreaths look so real you need to examine them carefully to notice any difference.

Marg and I enjoy making the wreath for the front door ourselves. It is not terribly difficult and we feel that the results are worth our efforts. Here are the supplies needed to make a wreath:

Base: Use a wire frame or a straw base, available at flower shops or craft stores.

Heavy twine: Loop twine through the wire or tie it around the straw base to make a loop to hang up the completed wreath.

Sturdy wire: Use wire to attach the greenery and the decorations. Florist pins and green floral tape work well with a straw base.

Greenery: You may choose traditional evergreen favourites such as pine or cedar. Some contemporary wreaths include less common greens such as ivy, eucalyptus branches, juniper and heather.

Ornaments: Today's wreaths are decorated with almost anything that adds colour—berries, pine cones, bells, dried flowers, and even items from the kitchen such as garlic, chilies, cinnamon sticks or dried fruit. Use ribbon to add a finishing touch.

Tools: You will need wire cutters for the wire and pruning shears to cut the greens.

To make the wreath:

Cut a piece of twine long enough to tie around the frame and to make a hanging loop when the wreath is finished.

Cut 3- to 6-inch lengths of greenery, wire the pieces together in bunches and attach them to the frame with wire or florist pins. Work in one direction so that the greens overlap each other. You can fill the entire wreath as you go. Another method is to work all the way around the outside, and then work the inside and finally the front surface.

When the greenery is securely in place, attach the ornaments by twisting a bit of wire around the branches.

Your wreath should have a theme. For example, a floral wreath incorporates different types of dried flowers. For a kitchen wreath, use fruits, vegetables and spices. A traditional wreath might be decorated with nuts, pinecones and berries. A wreath for a friend in Florida could includes starfish, shells and sand dollars. It's fun to be creative.

Add a beautiful bow of your favourite ribbon and your wreath is ready to hang.

AFTER A DAY OF MAKING wreaths or putting together jars of jams and fruits, its nice to have an easy supper that takes little time to prepare. The next few recipes fill the bill, and they are delicious as well.

Farfalle with Fresh Tomatoes and Basil

1 pound farfalle (bow tie) pasta

1 1/2 pounds ripe tomatoes, cored and cut into
   1/2-inch dice

1/4 cup extra-virgin olive oil

1/4 cup fresh basil leaves, coarsely chopped

1 small clove garlic, crushed

1/2 tsp salt or to taste

Grated Parmesan cheese (optional)

In a large pot of boiling salted water, cook pasta 10–12 minutes until *al dente* (firm to the bite), stirring occasionally to prevent pasta sticking.

Meanwhile in a large serving bowl, combine tomatoes, olive oil, basil, garlic and salt.

Drain the cooked pasta in a colander, and shake well. Add immediately to the tomato mixture and toss gently to combine. Sprinkle with Parmesan cheese, if desired, and serve immediately.

Serves 4

Add garlic bread and a green salad and you have a very quick supper.

THE NEXT PASTA RECIPE is versatile. I like to use chicken (either leftover or quick-cooked in the microwave) but you could use shrimp, sliced prosciutto, or thinly sliced beef.

Penne with Asparagus and Mushrooms

3–4 tsp extra-virgin olive oil (the amount depends on
*   whether you use chicken, shrimp, ham or beef)*

2 cups (6 ounces) sliced white mushrooms (button
*   mushrooms look nice but any white mushroom will do)*

1 tsp minced garlic (or 1 clove, sliced)

Salt and freshly ground pepper, to taste

1 boneless chicken breast or 2 slices prosciutto, cut in
slivers, or 6 shrimp, cooked, de-veined and sliced

1 pound penne pasta

1 bunch (about 1 pound) asparagus, trimmed and cut
diagonally into 1 1/2-inch pieces

1/2 cup shredded mozzarella cheese (optional)

1/2 cup grated Parmesan cheese

2 tbsp slivered fresh basil

In a large deep skillet heat olive oil over medium heat. Add mushrooms and cook stirring gently until mushrooms are golden and tender (about 10 minutes).

Add garlic, salt and pepper and cook for 2 more minutes. Add meat (or fish) and remove from heat.

In a large pot of boiling salted water, cook the pasta until almost firm to the bite (about 8 minutes). Add the asparagus, cook until tender (about 3 minutes), and drain.

Add the pasta and asparagus to the mixture in the skillet. Add the mozzarella and Parmesan cheese. Toss to mix and sprinkle with basil. Serve immediately.

Serves 6

SOUPS AND A SANDWICH ARE always a great hit for a fast dinner, and onion soup topped with toast and cheese is almost a meal in itself.

Super Onion Soup

1/2 cup butter
1/2 tsp freshly ground pepper
4 cups thinly sliced onions
1 1/2 cups dry white wine
3 cups water
1/4 cup chopped fresh parsley, firmly packed
2 tbsp soy sauce
1 tbsp Worcestershire sauce
1 tsp dried thyme
2 bay leaves
2 whole cloves
4 1/2-inch slices white bread, toasted
3 cups grated cheese (use a mixture of Gouda and Swiss)

In a large saucepan, over medium heat, melt butter until slightly browned. Add pepper and onions and cook, stirring constantly for 3–4 minutes or until the onions are coated in butter. Cook 30 minutes longer, stirring every 3–4 minutes until the onions are creamy, soft and light brown in colour.

Add the wine, and stir constantly with a wooden spoon for 3–4 minutes. Bring to a gentle boil and continue to stir for 2–3 minutes more. Add water, parsley, soy sauce, Worcestershire sauce, thyme, bay leaves and cloves and bring the soup to a full boil.

Reduce heat to medium low and cook for 30 minutes, or until the liquid is reduced by one fifth, stirring occasionally.

Remove from heat and let stand covered for 1 hour.

Preheat oven to 450°F. Divide the soup into four 1 1/2-cup ovenproof bowls, cover with the toasted bread and sprinkle with cheese. Bake 15 minutes until cheese is bubbling and has started to brown. Serve immediately.

I often serve this soup with hot rolls, or if I am really hungry, with a sandwich as well.

WHEN MY SON-IN-LAW Bruce wants to be helpful, he makes a skillet meal that he particularly enjoys. Since Bruce is a sausage lover, this dinner includes Kielbasa, a smoked Polish sausage that has a rich flavour.

Bruce's Kielbasa-Kale Dinner

1 tbsp light olive oil

1 pound Kielbasa sausage

2 pounds new potatoes, peeled and quartered

1 large onion, halved and sliced

2 tsp caraway seeds

1 tsp fennel seeds

1 tsp minced garlic

1 1/4 cups low-sodium chicken broth

1/4 tsp pepper

1 pound kale, shredded (about 6 cups)

2 tbsp chopped fresh parsley

In a large skillet, heat oil over medium high heat. Add Kielbasa and cook, turning occasionally, until browned—about 5 minutes. Transfer to a plate.

In the same skillet, combine the potatoes, onion, caraway, and fennel and garlic, cook until the onions soften, about 5 minutes. Add chicken broth and pepper, reduce heat to medium, and cook until potatoes begin to soften, about 5 minutes.

Meanwhile, cut the Kielbasa diagonally into 1/2-inch slices. Return to the skillet along with the kale. Cover and cook until potatoes are cooked through and the kale is tender, about 20-25 minutes. Stir in parsley and serve.

Serves 6

Yesterday hills and woods were gray
And boughs were bare and brown,
But all last night silently, silently,
Snow came down.

All night long over the fields,
Quiet and soft and slow
With a footprint, steadily, steadily
Walked in the snow

Now at dawn there is nothing but snow
Nothing but whiteness now,
Except the flame of a redbird's wing
On a feathery bough.

Nancy Byrd Turner

THE FIRST SNOW OF the season is so fresh and tranquil. It is God's blanket to comfort the earth and it is free for all to enjoy. There is something magical about an activity in the snow, whether it is skating on the pond for Justin and Jenny, snowmobiling for my grandson Marshall and his wife, or even a horse-drawn sleighride through the snow-covered pines. The cold weather also means that there will be many red noses and rosy cheeks coming in to warm up. I can't think of a better or more festive way to warm up than with a nice cup of hot cranberry cider.

Mulled Cranberry Cider

1 quart apple cider
1 quart cranberry-juice cocktail
1 tbsp firmly packed light brown sugar
2 3-inch cinnamon sticks
8 whole cloves
1/4 tsp ground nutmeg
8 8-inch cinnamon sticks (optional)
8 apple slices (optional)

In a 4 quart saucepan, combine the cider, cranberry juice, sugar, 3-inch cinnamon sticks, cloves and nutmeg and bring to a boil over high heat. Reduce heat to medium and simmer, covered, for 10 minutes. Ladle into mugs and garnish each one with an 8-inch cinnamon stick and a slice of apple, if desired.

IF YOU ASK MY GREAT grandchildren, no outdoor activity is complete unless they have a snack when they come in. Muffins are usually a big hit and these cheese and caraway muffins always produce requests for seconds.

Cheese and Caraway Muffins

2 cups flour, sifted
4 tsp baking powder
4 ounces sharp cheddar cheese, grated
2 tbsp caraway seeds
1/4 cup cooking oil
1 egg
1 1/2–2 cups milk
Pinch of salt

Preheat the oven to 400°F and grease a deep muffin pan.

Mix the sifted flour and baking powder in a large bowl. Add grated cheese and caraway seeds, then the oil, egg, salt and enough of the milk to form a dough the consistency of runny porridge. Don't over mix; the dough should be soft enough to pour. Spoon the mixture into well-greased deep muffin pans. Sprinkle the top of each muffin with shreds of cheese for a glossy finish.

Bake for 10–12 minutes, until well risen and golden brown.

Makes 1 dozen large muffins

Justin and Jenny love these muffins right out of the oven and Justin would happily eat three or four at one sitting (if his mother weren't watching).

LIGHTS HAVE BEEN A part of Christmas tradition for a very long time. For a thousand years people in Europe lit candles in their churches and their homes to welcome the Christ child, the Light of the World. Candles are still a popular decoration of the season, for mantle pieces, chandeliers, table centerpieces and they are used in many churches at evening services.

It is thought that Martin Luther was the first to decorate a tree with candles. According to legend, Luther was walking in the woods when he saw the stars in the sky twinkling between the branches of the fir trees. He found the sight to be so beautiful that he wanted to recreate it for his children. He placed small lighted tapers on a tree and a tradition was born.

The danger of fire prompted the invention of electric Christmas lights just three years after Thomas Edison invented the light bulb in 1882. The original bulbs for Christmas were simply smaller versions of household light bulbs. Before 1920, they were ball-shaped and coloured. As tree lights became less expensive, they became more common and they took on many shapes and forms. In the 1920s, lights in the shape of birds, flowers and fruit were popular. In the 1930s, miniature bulbs and bulbs that flashed became fashionable.

Then came bubble lights! From the mid-1940s right through the 1950s, bubble lights gained popularity unprecedented in the history of Christmas lighting. Noma Electric of New York first marketed these lights in 1945 and within a few years there were nearly 30 different types of bubble lights on the market.

For you young people, who have never seen a bubble light, I will explain. Bubble lights have three parts: a light bulb at the base, a sealed glass vial partially filled with methylene chloride sitting over the bulb, and an unbreakable plastic base housing the bulb. The heat from the bulb causes the methylene chloride to boil, producing bubbling action. Some bubble lights are still manufactured today, but they really can't compete with the bubble lights of yesteryear.

When we lived on the east coast, it was common practice in our small town to hold a decorating party the second week in December. Whole families would get together with neighbours to string lights, hang wreaths and set up crèches. It made for a most enjoyable day. In the evening, at a set time, every home would turn on their lights. It really was impressive.

We had a number of favourite dishes for these affairs. I will pass along a few of the most special.

Oyster and Corn Chowder

12 slices of bacon
1 large green pepper, diced
1 large red pepper, diced
2 onions, chopped
3 tbsp butter
3 potatoes, peeled
Salt and freshly ground pepper

1/2 tsp dried thyme

3 cups drained canned oysters (reserve liquid)

3 cups bottled clam juice or good strong fish stock

2 cups cream

1 tbsp Worcestershire sauce

2 cups frozen or canned sweet corn kernels

Snipped chives or green onions

Cook the bacon in a large heavy saucepan over medium heat until it begins to brown. Transfer to a paper towel.

Add peppers to the saucepan and cook until they begin to soften, about 5 minutes, stirring often. Transfer to another paper towel. Add the onions and butter to the pan. Reduce heat to medium low and cook until onions are tender. Add the potatoes and season with salt and pepper. Stir for 2 minutes. Mix in the thyme.

Add the reserved oyster juice, clam juice, Worcestershire sauce and cream to the pan and simmer until the potatoes are tender, about 20 minutes. Add the corn, bacon and peppers and simmer about 4 minutes.

Add the oysters, turn off the heat and let stand until the oysters begin to curl, about 1–2 minutes. Add salt and pepper to taste. Ladle soup into bowls and garnish with snipped chives or green onions.

Serves 6-8

George was very partial to dill so this bread was one of his favourites.

Dill Bread

1 package active dry yeast

1/4 cup warm water

1 cup lukewarm creamed cottage cheese

2 tbsp sugar

1 tbsp butter

1 tbsp finely chopped onion

1 tsp salt

1/4 tsp baking soda

1 egg

2 1/4–2 1/2 cups flour

Dissolve yeast in warm water. In a large bowl combine cottage cheese, sugar, butter, onion, dill seed, salt, soda and the egg. Stir, add yeast mixture, and continue stirring gradually. Stir in the flour to make a stiff dough and beat well; the mixture must be smooth.

Cover the bowl with a warm cloth and let rise in a warm place, away from drafts, for 50–60 minutes, or until the dough has doubled in bulk. Punch down and turn into a well buttered 1 1/2-quart round casserole (if you want a round loaf) or two regular bread loaf tins. Let the bread rise again for 30–40 minutes.

Bake at 350°F for 40–50 minutes.

Makes 1 round loaf or 2 small oblong loaves

COOKING FOR A LARGER group is not as difficult as it seems, particularly if you use a good sized ham and add potato pie and green beans with butter and lemon.

Maple Glazed Ham

1 12-pound fully cooked smoked whole ham

Whole cloves

1/2 cup dark brown sugar, firmly packed

1/4 cup maple syrup

Remove the skin and trim some of the fat from the ham, leaving about 1/4 inch fat. Insert whole cloves on ham in rows at 1 1/2 inch intervals.

Place ham on a rack in a large roasting pan. Insert meat thermometer into the centre of the ham; make sure that the pointed end of the thermometer does not touch the bone. Bake at 350°F for 3–3 1/2 hours. (Calculate 15–18 minutes per pound.) If the ham browns too quickly, cover with a tent of foil.

In a small bowl, mix brown sugar and maple syrup. About 30 minutes before the end of the baking time, spoon the maple glaze over the ham. Continue baking, basting occasionally, until the meat thermometer reaches 140°F.

When ham is done, place on a large platter; let stand 20 minutes for easier slicing.

Makes 24 servings

POTATO PIE IS AN old recipe from the Shakers, a religious group that originated in mid-18th-century England and later emigrated to the United States. Line pie tins with ordinary piecrust and fill with mashed potatoes seasoned with a little fried onion and summer savory. Dot with butter and add a top crust, or not, according to your choice. Bake for 20–30 minutes at 350°F. Serve hot. You will need 6 pies to serve 24.

Green Beans with Butter and Lemon

6 pounds fresh green beans
1/4 pound butter
3 tbsp lemon juice
1/4 tsp sea salt
Chopped parsley for garnish

Nip off the tips at each end of the beans and wash in cold water. I usually parboil the beans in advance; use 4 quarts of boiling water and 1 tsp salt for each pound of beans.

Rinse the beans in a colander under the hottest tap-water before dropping them into the boiling water. Add beans a few at a time so that the boiling is not interrupted. Do not cover the pot. Test the beans regularly for tenderness. When the beans are done, drain in the colander and run under cold water to stop the cooking process and refresh the beans. Spread on paper toweling and pat dry. If you parboil the beans ahead of time, wait until they cool and are completely dry before refrigerating in a covered bowl.

A few minutes before serving, melt the butter in a very large skillet. Toss in the beans and stir lightly for a minute or two over medium heat until the beans are heated through and coated with butter. Sprinkle with lemon juice and the sea salt. Toss the beans in the pan another few seconds and serve garnished with chopped parsley.

WE REMEMBER PARTICULARLY one Christmas decorating bee when my husband George was high on a ladder stringing lights on the chimney of the Robertson's home. Some of the young people were setting up the crèche below and a young man who was not paying close attention stepped backwards into the ladder, sending it sideways. Fortunately George had the presence of mind to grab on to the eavestrough as the ladder fell, but for several moments until the ladder was replaced, he dangled precariously from the second story. When George was once again on safe footing we actually laughed at the ridiculous picture that he had made. It might easily have been a scene in an Abbot and Costello film.

OUR FAMILY AND FRIENDS share a tradition that may be a part of your holiday season as well. It's our cookie exchange and this is how it works. Early in December each person involved makes 10–12 dozen cookies or squares, all the same kind. On a Saturday or Sunday afternoon everyone brings their cookies to one designated home. We usually share a cup of tea and a short visit before we begin to choose our cookies. Each person takes a half dozen of the different types of cookies until we have as many dozen as we brought with us. This way each of us has a wonderful and varied selection of Christmas treats to serve to family, friends or unexpected company during the season, without having to spend days in the kitchen.

As well, we usually attach copies of our recipes for the cookies and squares. This information is important for those who may have a restricted diet or severe allergies, but it also lets us bake particular favourites during the rest of the year.

The following recipes are family favourites collected over many years of exchanging goodies. I hope you and your families will find something special to enjoy.

Colourful Christmas Cookies

1 cup butter, softened

1 1/2 cups granulated sugar

3 eggs

1 tsp vanilla extract

1 tsp baking powder

1/2 tsp salt

4 cups all-purpose flour

Red and green food colouring

Cream butter and sugar until fluffy. Beat in the eggs until the mixture is well blended. Stir in vanilla, baking powder and salt. Mix in the flour, one cup at a time. Chill the dough at least 1 hour.

Preheat the oven to 375°F and grease a baking sheet. Divide the dough into 3 equal parts. With the food colouring, colour 1 part green and 1 part red; and leave the other part as it is. Roll out the dough to a thickness of about 1/8 inch.

Use cookie cutters to cut Christmas shapes such as stars, bells or trees out of one colour and cut larger circles out of another. Place the circles on a greased baking sheet, and cut the same Christmas shapes out of the circles. Remove the shapes and replace them with the same shape of a different colour.

Bake 6–10 minutes or until cookies are firm to the touch. Cool on rack and decorate with icing and candies.

Makes about 2 dozen large cookies

Although I have made these wooden spoon cookies for many years, I rarely have a chance to take them to the cookie exchange. Why? Because they are eaten as fast as I can make them.

Wooden Spoon Cookies

3/4 cup ground blanched almonds
1/2 cup margarine or butter, softened
1/2 cup sugar
1 tbsp all-purpose flour
1 tbsp whipping cream

Preheat oven to 350°F. Grease and flour 2 large cookie sheets. In a 2-quart saucepan, combine the ground almonds, margarine, sugar, flour and cream. Heat over low heat, stirring occasionally until the margarine melts. Keep mixture warm over very low heat.

Drop batter by rounded teaspoons about 3 inches apart on the cookie sheet. Do not place more than 6 cookies on a sheet at one time as the cookies must be rolled quickly after baking before they harden.

Bake cookies 5–7 minutes, until the edges are lightly browned and the centres are golden. Let cookies remain on the cookie sheet 30–60 seconds until the edges are just set.

With a flexible metal spatula, flip the cookies over so that the lacy texture will be on the outside after rolling. Working as quickly as possible, roll each cookie around the handle of a wooden spoon, then remove to a wire rack to cool. (If the cookies become too hard to roll, return them briefly to the oven to soften, then remove and roll.)

Repeat this process until all of the batter has been used.

Makes about 3 dozen cookies

Peanut Butter Chocolate Bars

1 cup smooth or chunky peanut butter

6 tbsp butter or margarine, softened

3/4 cup packed brown sugar

1/2 cup granulated sugar

1 tsp vanilla extract

3 eggs

1 cup all-purpose flour

2 cups (11 ounces) Nestlé mild chocolate morsels,
  or milk chocolate chips

1 cup coloured sugar or small coloured candies

  (optional decoration)

Preheat the oven to 350°F and grease a 9 × 13-inch baking pan. Beat the peanut butter, butter, brown sugar and granulated sugar in a large mixing bowl until creamy. Beat in the eggs, then beat in the flour. Stir in 3/4 cup of the chocolate morsels or chips. Spread mixture into the greased pan.

Bake for 20–25 minutes, or until edges are lightly browned. Remove from the oven and immediately sprinkle with remaining chocolate pieces. Let stand for 5 minutes while the chocolate pieces melt, then spread the melted chocolate evenly.

Sprinkle coloured sugar or candies over melted chocolate (optional). Cool in the pan or on a wire rack.

These squares are very rich so they should be cut in small pieces. We usually cut about 30 pieces per pan.

MY FRIEND MARIA ANDREOLI made these Italian Christmas cookies for our exchange several years ago and they have become family favourites. The toasted pine nuts (pignoli) give them such a distinctive flavour.

Italian Christmas Cookies

2 3/4 cups all-purpose flour

1 1/4 cups granulated sugar

1 cup butter-flavour shortening or plain shortening

2 tsp cream of tartar

1 tsp baking soda

1/4 tsp salt

3/4 tsp anise extract

3 large eggs

6 ounces pine nuts (pignoli), toasted

In a large bowl, combine flour, sugar, shortening, cream of tartar, baking soda, salt, anise extract and 2 eggs. With mixer at low speed, beat until well blended, occasionally scraping the bowl with a rubber spatula.

Preheat oven to 375°F.

In a small bowl, beat the remaining egg with a fork. Place toasted pine nuts in another small bowl. Roll the dough into 1-inch balls. Dip half of each ball into the beaten egg then press the same side into the pine nuts, flattening slightly. Place cookies, nut side up, about 2 inches apart on large ungreased cookie sheets.

Bake for 12 minutes or until the edges are golden. With a spatula remove cookies to a wire rack to cool. Store in a tightly covered container.

Makes about 3 1/2 dozen

It's the little things in life that count,
The things of every day;
Just the simple things that we can do,
The kind words we can say.

The little things like a friendly smile
For those who may be sad,
The clasp of a hand or kindly deed
To help make someone glad.
A knock on the door of lonely homes,
Or flowers bright and gay,
For someone to whom you might bring cheer
With just a small bouquet.
Just the little greetings here and there
On which so much depends,
The little pleasures that all can share,
The joy of making friends.

THIS LITTLE POEM IS an excellent reminder to us during the holiday season. For many people, Christmas is not the happiest time of year. For shut-ins or friends confined to nursing homes, it can be a time when they feel forgotten. It is important to make time in our busy schedules to stop in with a card or perhaps a poinsettia with a Christmas candle. "It's the little things in life that count." Make someone else's day a little happier and you are sure to have brightened your own.

With the holidays comes the inevitable task of playing hostess to the many friends and family who come from near and far to extend holiday greetings. Hors d'oeuvres and snacks are as popular as any feast. Holiday get-togethers seem to go hand in hand with what George used to call "munching." Here are a few of my new favourite snack recipes, sure to please guests during the holiday season, or any other time of year.

Bruschetta

1 14-inch loaf of Italian bread

2 cups chopped, seeded, fresh tomato

1/2 cup finely chopped onion

4 cloves garlic, pressed

4 tsp olive oil

1 tbsp balsamic vinegar

1/2 tsp ground black pepper

Grated cheddar and Parmesan cheese (optional)

Heat oven to 350°F. Combine tomato, onion, garlic, oil, vinegar and pepper in a bowl and let sit. Cut the ends from the bread. Slice the remaining loaf end to end and then crosswise into 24 pieces 1/2 inch thick. Place bread slices on an ungreased baking sheet and bake until lightly toasted. Spread tomato mixture on bread to cover surface, piling as high as desired. Sprinkle with cheese, and broil just long enough to melt the cheese. Arrange bruschetta on a platter and serve.

For those who may be thinking of their waistline this season, this recipe is low in fat and contains no cholesterol.

THIS NEXT RECIPE SEEMS to appeal to the younger crowd, although I enjoy it very much as well.

Six-Layer Mexican Dip and Chips

1 package Philadelphia cream cheese

1 jar chunky salsa dip (mild or medium, to your taste)

1 package guacamole dip (pre-made is easier, but you can
    make your own with avocados and guacamole dip mix)

1 can refried beans (optional)

3 green onions, finely chopped

1 1/2 cups grated cheddar and mozzarella cheese mixed

1 large bag tortilla chips (the baked variety have less fat)

Preheat oven to 350°F. In a deep glass pie pan or a lasagna pan, layer the ingredients in the following order: Spread cream cheese over the bottom of pan, covering it completely in an even thickness. Spread guacamole on top of cream cheese. Add a layer of salsa, about 1/2 inch thick, followed by a layer of refried beans (if using), and sprinkle green onions on top. Cover with grated cheese.

Bake just long enough to melt the cheeses. Serve hot as a dip with tortilla chips. Keep plenty of serviettes on hand as this dish can be quite messy. (I don't think I would choose to serve it in a room with a white Indian carpet.)

THIS NEXT RECIPE IS nice to have on hand as it is a quick and easy vegetarian snack. You can buy hummus in most grocery stores, or you can make your own with chick peas, garlic and oil.

Hummus and Pita Dip

1 quart fresh hummus

8-10 thin pita breads, cut into triangular sections

grated cheddar cheese (to taste)

carrots and celery

Preheat oven to 350°F. Place pita sections on an un-greased cookie sheet and bake 8–10 minutes or until lightly toasted. Sprinkle with grated cheddar cheese and broil until cheese is melted. Serve with hummus dip and carrots and celery on the side.

THIS QUICK, FESTIVE APPETIZER or "munchy" has a great combination of flavours.

Brie and Roasted Garlic Appetizer

2 whole garlic bulbs

1 12-ounce round of brie cheese at room temperature

1 6-ounce jar roasted red peppers, drained (or 2 to 3 whole roasted peppers) cut in bite-sized strips

Small slices of bread or mini pitas

Preheat oven to 375°F. Remove most of the outer skin of the garlic bulbs, leaving the last couple of layers; do not peel down to the clove itself. Place garlic on a baking sheet and bake for about 45 minutes or until cloves are soft.

Place the brie in the centre of a serving plate. Separate the roasted garlic cloves and place around the Brie. Arrange peppers and bread on the plate. The circular display looks much like a Christmas wreath.

To eat, spread a bread slice with brie, squeeze on roasted garlic and top with a slice of roasted pepper.

ALTHOUGH IT SEEMS THAT our time is taken up with tasks to get ready for the "big day," we need only think back to the days of the early settlers to realize how much easier our life is now. In those days the chores were divided; men and women had specific jobs to tackle before Christmas Day.

Women's Pre-Christmas Tasks:

- Clean the house
- Wash the tablecloths, rugs and curtains
- Press the best quilts
- Make new clothes for every member of the family to wear at the Christmas parties
- Make jams and preserves
- Choose the best vegetables and fruits and store them separately to be used only at Christmas
- Prepare pies and cakes which can be made ahead of time
- Prepare the sausages and roasts
- Make soups
- Make mincemeat for pies
- Prepare the plum pudding

- Set aside the best spices and herbs
- Pluck feathers from the goose, save for pillows
- Prepare a Christmas hamper for the minister and his family

Men's Pre-Christmas Tasks:

- Cut firewood for the fireplace
- Bring the flour home from the mill
- Hunt or slaughter the animals and birds for roasting
- Prepare the sausage, bacon and roasts for cooking
- Repair, paint and varnish the sleighs
- Polish the Christmas sleigh bells
- Check the harness
- Air the bear, wolf and moose blankets in the sleighs
- Brush down the horses
- Run errands for the women
- Clear the road to the church
- Chop evergreens for decorations

I LIKE TO INVITE CLOSE friends over for a special dinner during the festive season. Although I don't do it often, I put a lot of effort into making dishes that are spectacular to look at or to taste—or both. Here then is an Edna McCann dinner menu for special friends.

Cranberry Punch

2 cups cranberries

2 cups water

1 cup sugar

Juice of 3 lemons

Juice of 1 lime

1 quart gingerale, chilled

Red and green cherries

Ice, as desired

Combine the cranberries, water and sugar and cook until the berries are reduced to a pulp. Allow the mixture to cool, then strain the liquid into a punch bowl and add the remaining ingredients.

Serves 6–8

Baby Quiche with Lemon Shrimp

3 sheets ready-rolled puff pastry

1 1/2 cups tiny cooked shrimp

1 cup cream

4 large eggs, lightly beaten

2 tsp finely grated lemon rind

1 tsp finely chopped parsley

Freshly ground black pepper and salt to taste

Preheat the oven to 400°F.

Cut circles from the pastry using a fluted 2 1/2-inch cutter. Press into mini muffin tins. Divide shrimps between the pastry cups. Combine cream, eggs, lemon rind, parsley, salt and pepper and spoon over shrimps. Do not fill more than 3/4 full.

Bake for 10 minutes or until puffed and golden brown.

Makes approximately 36 quiches

I like to refrigerate leftovers. They can be eaten cold or reheated in the microwave.

THE SOUP IS NICE because it isn't heavy. The secret of its elegance is in the serving; demitasse cups add that touch of class.

Christmas Soup

1 46-ounce can V-8 juice

1 11-ounce can beef consommé

2 bay leaves

4 cloves

Dash of Worcestershire sauce

Dash of Tabasco sauce

Combine all the ingredients and simmer for 1 hour. Serve hot in demitasse cups.

Serves 8

I LOVE LAMB AND this recipe, sent to me by Gavin McBurney of Australia, is one of my favourites of all time. It looks absolutely magnificent on the plate and it tastes every bit as wonderful as it looks.

Garlic Roasted Lamb Chops with Cranberry Port Sauce

Lamb rib chops (allow 4–5 chops per person depending on the size of the chops)

6 large cloves garlic, crushed

1 cup red wine

2 cups oil

3 tbsp dried rosemary

Cranberry Port Sauce (recipe follows)

Combine garlic, wine, oil and rosemary in a saucepan, and bring to a boil, stirring constantly. Cool, strain out the rosemary, and pour over the chops. Allow to marinate at least 6 hours.

Drain the marinade off the chops, then roast in a moderately hot oven (about 375°F). Do not overcook; chops are best when left slightly pink. (You can pre-cook the chops and keep oven warm.)

Ladle spoonfuls of cranberry sauce onto warmed dinner plates. Arrange the chops in the sauce and garnish with a small sprig of fresh rosemary.

Cranberry Port Sauce

1 pound cranberries (fresh or frozen)

1 cup port

1/2 cup red wine

1/2 cup water

2 tbsp sugar

2 tbsp arrowroot

Combine all ingredients except the arrowroot and boil for 10 minutes. Strain the mixture and return to the saucepan. Mix the arrowroot with a little water, spoon in a little of the cranberry mixture, then add to the saucepan, whisking continuously until the liquid thickens and clears. (The continuous whisking prevents a glue-like consistency.)

Serve immediately with lamb chops.

TO ME, WILD RICE is the perfect accompaniment for the lamb. The pine nuts add another special touch.

Wild Rice with Herbs and Pine Nuts

4 tbsp unsalted butter

1/2 cup chopped onions

1 stalk celery, minced

1/2 pound mushrooms, sliced

1 tart apple, cored and finely chopped

2 cups long grain wild rice

4 cups chicken stock (or chicken bouillon)

1/2 cup pine nuts

1/2 cup chopped mixed fresh herbs (if available, use mint, parsley, sage, marjoram, tarragon) or 1/4 cup dried herbs

Salt and pepper to taste

Melt the butter in a saucepan. Add the onions and celery and cook for 7 minutes. Add mushrooms and apple and cook 3 minutes longer. Stir in rice and cook for 5 minutes over moderate heat.

Stir in stock or bouillon and cook for 25 minutes or until the rice is tender and the liquid is absorbed. Stir in nuts and herbs. Taste and adjust seasonings.

Makes 8 half-cup servings

Buttered Carrots

1 1/4 pounds baby carrots
1/2 tsp salt
1 tsp sugar
1/8 cup butter
1/4 cup chopped fresh parsley

If the carrots are in small bags, they are likely peeled. If not, peel the carrots and cut them lengthwise in half. Boil about 1/2 quart water in the teakettle.

Combine carrots, salt, sugar and butter in saucepan. Pour boiling water over the carrots to a depth of about 2 inches. Cook, covered, over low heat for about 15 minutes or until carrots are tender. Remove cover and cook for another 5 minutes to reduce liquid.

Turn into a serving dish and sprinkle with chopped parsley before serving.

NO DINNER IN OUR home is complete without dessert, and at this time of year there seems to be an endless array of yummy treats to choose from. Eggnog is a taste that we seldom enjoy except at Christmas, so I like to have it whenever I can. This crème brulée is sure to be a hit.

Eggnog Crème Brulée

10 egg yolks
4 cups 35% cream
1 vanilla bean, split in half with centre scraped out
1/4 tsp grated fresh nutmeg
1 cup granulated sugar
pinch of ground cloves
2 1/2 tsp rum

Preheat oven to 300°F.

In a medium bowl, stir egg yolks together with a rubber spatula. In medium saucepan, over high heat, combine cream, vanilla bean, nutmeg, 1/2 cup sugar and cloves. Bring to a boil. Pour slowly over egg yolks, while stirring constantly with a spatula. Do not whisk. Strain immediately. Skim off any foam and stir in the rum.

Place 10 3-inch ramekins in a deep baking pan filled with water. The water should reach half way up the sides of the ramekins. Divide the egg yolk mixture between ramekins and cover pan with foil.

Bake on the middle rack of the oven about 50-60 minutes or until slightly soft in the centre when shaken. Remove ramekins from the water and cover with plastic wrap. Do not let wrap touch the surface. Set aside to chill.

Prior to serving, in a heavy bottom saucepan over medium-high heat, cook the remaining 1/2 cup sugar 3–4 minutes until sugar turns a dark amber. Remove from the heat and quickly pour 1 tsp of hot sugar over each custard.

Serves 10

Extra custards will keep in the refrigerator—but not long if your family spots them.

It came upon the midnight clear,
That glorious song of old,
From angels bending near the earth
To touch their harps of gold,
"Peace on the earth, good will to men
From heaven's all gracious King!"
The world in solemn stillness lay
To hear the angels sing.

Edmund Hamilton Sears

HOW I LOVE TO sing the old traditional Christmas carols. Often at this time of year the Sunday school children join us in the church. The sound of their voices added to our ours gives the carols a unique and joyful sound. What better than children's voices to welcome the birth of a baby.

The origins of the Christmas carol are mixed. Some etymologists believe the word 'carol' comes from the Greek and Latin word *chorus*, while others suggest the Latin word *corolla* (meaning crown, coronet, or garland) is the more likely root. Certainly the ancient Greeks performed circle dances. The name for the flute player who accompanied these dances is *choraules*. The ancient Romans also included dances into their Saturnalia festivals and other celebrations.

In medieval Britain and France, the carol or *carole* was a courtly or popular dance song. Gradually the dance aspect lessened; carols with religious as well as secular texts began to appear, and carol singing became established in churches as well as homes and fair grounds. The earliest surviving printed collection of English carols was published in 1521 by Wynkyn de Worde, an English printer of French origin.

In the 16th century, the changes brought about by the Reformation led to a decline of the carol, and during the 17th century religious festivities came under pressure from Puritan reformers. So strong was the influence of the church that religious carols almost completely disappeared.

The 19th century saw the publication of a number of collections of carols in England and America. This renewed interest led to new carols being composed and old ones being rediscovered.

Carols became very popular with music-loving Victorians and it became a Christmas Eve tradition for groups of singers to tour the streets singing such popular carols as *Angels from the Realms of Glory* or *Good King Wenceslas*.

The affluent saw caroling as a means of doling out charity. Homeowners often paid the singers with coins or gifts of fruit or nuts. Carolers might also be invited into the homes of the wealthy for a warming glass of punch or wassail and hot mince pies.

When we lived on Canada's east coast, we would often welcome groups of carol singers into our home. Although caroling wasn't as popular when we were in the north, it seems as if more and more Canadians are practicing this tradition nowadays.

WHEN CAROLERS COME TO our door, we like to have a variety of snacks and hot drinks to share with them. The next few recipes seem to be quite popular with both young and old.

Special Hot Chocolate

1 cup water

8 ounces chocolate, roughly chopped

5 cups milk

3 tbsp brown sugar

1/2 cup cream

1/2 tsp cinnamon

Pinch of nutmeg

8 long cinnamon sticks (for garnish)

Heat the water, add the chocolate and stir until dissolved. Add the milk and bring slowly to the boil. Stir in the sugar. Lightly whip the cream with the cinnamon and the nutmeg. Pour the hot chocolate into eight mugs and top with a dollop of cream. Serve with a cinnamon stick in each mug to stir the cream.

FOR THE ADULTS IN the group, Bruce makes a delicious mulled wine.

Hot Mulled Wine

1 cinnamon stick

4 whole cloves

1/2 tsp grated nutmeg

1 tbsp sliced lemon peel (zest removed)

1/2 cup sherry

1 bottle red wine

Sugar to taste

Place the spices and lemon peel in a large saucepan, barely cover with water. Simmer for 30 minutes. Strain, and add sherry, wine and sugar. Heat but do not boil.

Serves 6

SOME OF THE EASIEST snacks to share with visitors are crackers, potato chips, or vegetables served with an assortment of dips or pâtés. These next few selections are "tried, tested and true" and sure to make your home a most popular place for carolers.

Cheddar Cheese Dip

2 cups (about 1/2 pound) grated old cheddar cheese

1/2 cup low-fat mayonnaise

1 can condensed cheese soup

1/4 tsp onion powder

1 tsp parsley flakes

1 tsp lemon juice

Combine all ingredients and refrigerate in serving bowls. Serve with crackers.

Makes about 3 cups

Shrimp Avocado Dunk

2 ripe avocados

1 cup sour cream

2 tbsp chili sauce

1/2 tsp salt

1 cup cooked shrimp, chopped into small pieces

Remove the skins and the pits from the avocados and mash the fruit in a bowl with a fork. Blend in the sour cream, chili sauce, and salt, then fold in the shrimp. Refrigerate until needed.

To serve, place dip bowl in the centre of a tray and surround with potato chips, nachos, pretzels and crackers.

Makes 2 1/2 cups

A DEAR YOUNG FRIEND of mine, Bonnie Gosse, gave me this recipe for salmon dip. Bonnie is very health conscious and has done her best to try to make me more aware of my eating habits in the hope, I suppose, of "teaching an old dog new tricks." I expect that I am probably one of Bonnie's miserable failures, but I do love this next recipe so I hope this is a small measure of comfort to her.

Super Salmon Dip

1 7-ounce can red Sockeye salmon, drained, with
*   bones removed*
8 ounces light cream cheese, softened
1 tsp minced garlic
1 tsp lemon juice
1 tbsp Worcestershire sauce
1 tbsp chopped parsley
Parsley sprigs for garnish

Lightly mash the salmon with a fork to break into small pieces. Place softened cream cheese in a medium sized bowl. Add salmon, garlic, lemon juice, Worcestershire sauce, and parsley. Blend together well with a fork.

Cover bowl with plastic and refrigerate until about an hour before serving. Decorate serving bowl with sprigs of parsley and serve with a basket of low-fat wheat thin crackers.

THIS NEXT DIP IS VERY attractive and delicious with crackers or small pieces of toast at holiday time.

Spiced Cranberry Nut Dip

2 cups fresh cranberries

1 orange, quartered and seeded

1/4 cup water

1 cup sugar

1/8 tsp cinnamon

1/8 tsp nutmeg

1/8 tsp allspice

1/2 cup salted peanuts, chopped

Put cranberries and orange through a food chopper. Combine in a saucepan with water, sugar and spices and cook over medium heat until thickened, about 15 minutes. Stir in peanuts. For an even smoother consistency, place all ingredients in a blender and blend about two minutes, stopping the motor and shifting the contents once or twice.

MY HUSBAND GEORGE LOVED blue cheese—the stronger the cheese, the better he liked it. This dip for vegetables was one of his favourites.

Blue Cheese Dip

1/2 pint sour cream

1 tsp instant minced green onion

3 ounces blue cheese

Place sour cream and onion in a bowl. Crumble blue cheese into the bowl and mix well. Serve with a selection of vegetables; my favourites are carrots, celery, mushrooms, slices of red, green and yellow peppers, cauliflower and broccoli.

THIS GOOSE LIVER PÂTÉ is delicious but also pretentious enough to serve at the most elegant of cocktail parties.

Goose Liver Pâté Speciale

4 tins goose liver pâté (about 8–9 ounces)

16 ounces Philadelphia cream cheese

1 small onion, grated

1/4 cup bourbon

1/2 tbsp Worcestershire sauce

Salt and pepper to taste

1 envelope unflavoured gelatin

1 can consommé

2 hard-boiled eggs

Watercress for garnish

Mix the pâté and cream cheese together; add the grated onion and then the bourbon, Worcestershire sauce and salt and pepper.

Dissolve the gelatin in 1/2 of the consommé and heat. Add the other half of the consommé. Mix 2 tbsp of consommé into the pâté mixture.

Wet a 1-quart decorative mould with water, and set in a bowl of ice. Spread a layer of consommé over the bottom of the mould, then a layer of sliced hard boiled egg, then more consommé, and let it set over the ice. Add the pate mixture, then the rest of the consommé and refrigerate for about 4 hours.

To serve, turn out on a very cold platter and garnish with watercress. Serve with hot toast triangles.

ALTHOUGH I ALWAYS ASSOCIATE caroling with snow and visions of people in Victorian outfits, Christmas carols are sung all over the world. My dear friend Emily, who winters in Florida, sent me a video from her condominium complex last winter. How interesting it was to see Emily and her friends in summer attire singing the beautiful *Silent Night*

in front of palm trees decorated with miniature lights. In the background I could see sailboats covered in lights sailing in the Christmas Boat Parade, so popular in the St. Petersburg area. It certainly gives Christmas a different look.

MY SON-IN-LAW PUT THE Christmas seals on the last of our cards to be mailed today and another task is completed.

The annual Christmas Seal campaign, a program of the Canadian Lung Association, had its origins in 1907. Emily Bissell, a social worker, was struggling to keep a small tuberculosis clinic open in Delaware. Learning about a special Christmas stamp that was issued in Denmark to raise money for needy children, Emily designed her own stamp showing a holly wreath and the words Merry Christmas. She sold the stamps in packets with the message:

> *Put this stamp*
> *On every Christmas letter*
> *Help the tuberculosis fight*
> *And make the New Year better.*

Her stamps raised more than enough money to keep the small sanitarium open and with the extra money the National Tuberculosis Association was born. Today the Canadian Lung Association still uses Christmas Seals to raise funds to fight lung disease.

WHEN MY GREAT-GRANDCHILDREN come to visit, I like to serve dishes that I know they will enjoy. I have found that even the most finicky eaters are happy to help themselves when these favourites are served.

Dynamite Drumsticks

1/2 cup apricot preserves

1/4 cup teriyaki sauce

1 tbsp dark brown sugar

1 tsp corn starch

1 tsp cider vinegar

1/4 tsp salt

11 medium chicken drumsticks (about 3 pounds),
   skin removed

Preheat oven to 425°F. In a large bowl, use a wire whisk to mix apricot preserves, teriyaki sauce, brown sugar, cornstarch, vinegar and salt until blended. Add chicken and toss to coat.

Spoon chicken and sauce into a medium jelly roll pan (about 10 × 15 inches). Bake for 15 minutes. Remove from the oven. Using a pastry brush, brush the chicken with the sauce in the pan. Cook chicken 15–20 minutes longer brushing with sauce every 5 minutes.

Remove chicken from oven and brush once more with sauce. Allow to cool in the pan for about 10 minutes before serving. Place in a serving dish and spoon remaining sauce over the chicken.

Be sure to have plenty of paper napkins or wet cloths handy as these drumsticks can be very messy! Small children will usually eat one drumstick each, but the teenagers in our family have been known to eat 4 or 5 apiece.

Macaroni and Cheese

8 ounces corkscrew pasta

3 cups milk

1 1/2 tbsp cornstarch

1/4 tsp salt

Dash of ground nutmeg

1/4 cup grated Parmesan cheese

4 ounces sharp cheddar cheese, grated (about 1 cup)

Preheat oven to 375°F. Cook pasta as the label directs in boiling salted water; drain.

Meanwhile, in a medium saucepan, use a wire whisk to mix milk, cornstarch, salt and nutmeg until blended. Cook over medium heat until mixture thickens slightly and comes to a boil, whisking frequently. Remove saucepan from heat. Gradually whisk in Parmesan cheese until the cheese melts and the sauce is smooth.

Spoon pasta into a shallow 13 × 9-inch glass baking dish. Pour sauce over the pasta and stir to mix well. Sprinkle the cheddar cheese over the pasta but do not stir. Bake uncovered for 25 minutes or until hot and bubbling.

Serves 4-6

I DON'T KNOW WHAT it's like in your home, but in ours cooked vegetables are not very high on the "please may I have more" list. The children will, however, eat a wide variety of raw vegetables with a mixture of dips.

Vegetables for Dipping

Carrots, celery, green pepper strips, cauliflower, broccoli, sliced cucumber

Peanut Butter–Ginger Dip

3/4 cup creamy peanut butter
1/3 cup very hot tap water
1/4 cup honey
4 tsp soy sauce
1 tsp grated fresh ginger (peel before grating)

In a medium bowl with a wire whisk, blend all the ingredients together until smooth. Let the dip sit at room temperature until ready to serve; the mixture will harden if refrigerated.

Makes 1 1/4 cups

Onion Sour Cream Dip

8 ounces sour cream
1 package dried onion soup mix
1/2 tsp Worcestershire sauce

Blend all the ingredients together. Refrigerate until ready to serve.

DESSERTS ARE ALWAYS ENJOYED. This festive dessert could not be more simple. Here's all you need:

1 quart vanilla ice cream

2 candy canes

Break the candy canes into small pieces. Soften the ice cream slightly and mix in the candy cane bits. Refreeze until ready to serve.

I SERVE THIS DESSERT to the children when we get together to make gingerbread houses.

For several years now, our family has followed the instructions given in the December issue of *Good Housekeeping* to replicate prize winning gingerbread houses selected from entries from across North America. Those of us in the "older generation" work together on the house that will be our centerpiece, but we also provide ingredients for the children to make their own miniature houses.

Although we call them "gingerbread" houses, they are really cookie houses. If you have grandchildren, or great-grandchildren visiting during the holiday season this wonderful activity will keep them occupied for hours, particularly if you suggest that they make a "town" with a variety of decorated homes.

Cookie House

Assorted large crackers and cookies: Use varieties such as square Graham wafers, Social Teas, or Wasa Crisps for building and try sugar wafers, scalloped butter cookies or chocolate wafers for decorating.

1 batch of Thick Royal Icing (see below) or one tub of ready-to-use Ornamental Frosting (not ready-to-use frosting), usually available wherever you can buy cake decorating equipment.

Assorted decorations including colourful candies, pretzel sticks, small ice cream cones, Smarties, gum drops, miniature candy canes, mini-coloured chicklets, and tiny cinnamon hearts.

Thick Royal Icing

4 cups confectioners' sugar

2 egg whites

1 1/2 tsp fresh lemon juice, strained

Using a wooden spoon, stir about half of the sugar into the egg whites. Add the lemon juice and beat the mixture with a wooden spoon until it is thoroughly blended. Add the remaining sugar a little at a time, beating well after each addition. Continue to beat for 15 minutes or until the mixture is smooth and creamy.

The icing can be used immediately or kept for about 30 minutes if covered with a damp cloth. If kept longer, the icing will begin to set.

ASSEMBLE HOUSES OR OTHER structures using large crackers or cookies, attaching each piece with Royal Icing. Spread icing on the edges of the cookies to be joined and hold together for a few minutes until set. (If young children are involved, you might choose to assemble a few houses before they arrive and let them do the decorating only).

Decorate as desired. Decorations can be easily attached with Royal Icing. Here are a few ideas:

Make a log cabin by icing the outer walls and attaching pretzel sticks.

Make a church steeple with an iced sugar wafer and a pretzel cross. Trim wafers for the doors of the church and make stained glass windows by cutting small pieces from gum drops.

Chocolate wafers make a great roof. Spread icing generously on the roof and then overlap the wafers slightly, starting at the bottom.

Use ice cream cones to make castle turrets and candy canes to make lampposts. Candy canes also make great sleigh runners for Santa's sleigh. The sleigh can be made of wafers.

Pine cones with dabs of frosting and tiny cinnamon hearts can serve as decorated trees for your village.

With food and imagination there is no end to the enjoyment that children can have with this activity. Even the teenagers who, at first, offer to help the little ones, usually wind up making their own house or village.

ANOTHER ACTIVITY THAT WE enjoy in our family is "Christmas Movie Night" (or nights, as there are so many outstanding seasonal films). Often my grandson Fred or his wife June will call and say "Saturday is movie night—hope you can come." Many members of the family have been known to cancel other plans so as not to miss the evening.

My favourite of the old films is the 1951 version of Charles Dickens' *A Christmas Carol*. Alistair Sims was critically acclaimed for his brilliant portrayal of Mr. Scrooge, and even the youngsters in the family love this most famous of Christmas films.

It's a Wonderful Life, the 1946 film starring Jimmy Stewart and Donna Reed, is based on the short story *The Greatest Gift* by Philip Van Doren Stern. Jimmy Stewart, as George Bailey, is the manager of a small savings and loan company in a small town in the United States. When he questions his worth in this world, an angel appears to save him and raise his Christmas spirits.

The 1947 version of *Miracle on 34th Street* really appeals to the youngsters in the family and I could watch *Holiday Inn* over and over again if only to hear Bing Crosby's immortal crooning of *White Christmas*.

When we all get together, it's fun to have an easy dinner so that everyone can enjoy the evening without interruption. Lasagna with a salad and hot herb buttered bread is a meal everyone loves.

Extra Easy Lasagna

1 pound lean ground beef
3 cups of your favourite spaghetti sauce
9 oven-ready lasagna noodles

1/2 pound mushrooms, sliced

1 container (about 15 ounces) ricotta cheese

2 tbsp Italian seasoning

2 eggs

1/2 cup Parmesan cheese

2 cups shredded mozzarella cheese

In a 1-inch skillet over medium high heat, cook beef until browned, stirring to separate meat. Spoon off fat. Add mushrooms and spaghetti sauce. Heat through, stirring occasionally.

In a bowl, mix together ricotta cheese, eggs, Parmesan cheese and Italian seasoning.

In a 13 × 9 × 2-inch pan spread 1 cup of the meat sauce on the bottom. Top with 3 lasagna noodles. Cover noodles with the ricotta cheese mixture and 1 cup mozzarella cheese. Top this with 3 lasagna noodles. Cover noodles with all but 1/2 cup of the meat sauce. Top with last 3 noodles and cover with the remaining sauce and shredded mozzarella.

Cover with foil and bake at 375°F for 45 minutes. Uncover and bake 15 minutes more or until cheese looks bubbly. Let stand 10 minutes before serving. Makes 8–10 servings.

SALADS ARE VERY POPULAR in our household, providing almost every dinner with added vegetables.

This tradition began when my daughters were very young. They possessed a strong dislike of cooked vegetables, especially green ones. I became very familiar with all their tricks to dispose of unwanted items, from feeding the dog under the table, to stuffing them in their cheeks and excusing themselves to the bathroom to spit them out.

One of the more humorous moments I remember came on a hot spring afternoon. I was doing my usual spring clean-up when I noticed a rather pungent smell emanating from the kitchen. Search as I did, I could not trace the source of the foul odor. Eventually I zeroed in on the far corner of the eating area of the kitchen. We had a decorative milk jug standing in the corner, acting as a plant holder. As I lifted the potted plant from its stand, I was overcome with nausea. Then it dawned on me; apparently, for some months, my girls had been lifting the plant, and disposing of the unwanted greens in the jug, then replacing the plant. Since it was Julia's task to water the indoor plants, I had no need to be close to the planter. When the time came....Wow! George and I had a great deal of difficulty deciding who would be able to discipline the girls without laughing.

For whatever reason, the girls would eat salad with almost any vegetables included, so I found it easier to make a salad than to worry about cooking vegetables and enduring the inevitable arguments.

When my daughter Julia provided this spinach salad recipe for our last movie night, I reminded her of her trick so long ago.

Spunky Spinach Salad

2 packages fresh spinach
4 small green apples, sliced
1 1/2 cups chopped pecans

1 1/2 cups raisins

2 large avocados, peeled, pitted and sliced

1 cup sun-dried tomatoes

Your favourite herb vinaigrette dressing

Wash spinach thoroughly. Shake off excess water and break in pieces in a large salad bowl. Add apples, avocados, pecans, raisins and sun-dried tomatoes. Slowly add dressing and toss lightly, just enough to cover salad.

Serves 8–10

Herb-Buttered French Bread

1 loaf French bread

Softened butter

Your favourite herbs

Garlic powder (optional)

Slice down through the bread crosswise, almost to the bottom of the loaf. Make cuts about 1 inch apart.

Mix herbs into the softened butter along with a little garlic powder. Hold the slices apart and spread with the butter mixture.

Place the loaf on a piece of aluminum foil. Bring foil up around the loaf, folding the ends to seal but leaving a small opening in the top. Bake at 350°F for about 15 minutes.

This bread will be hot and buttery with a crisp crust—delicious!

RICE PUDDING WITH RAISINS can be prepared ahead of time and then cooked while the family eats dinner in front of the television. I prefer the pudding warm but you can also cook the pudding early in the day and refrigerate until serving time.

Rice Pudding with Raisins

2 1/2 cups milk

1/4 tsp salt

3/4 cup granulated sugar

2 tbsp softened butter

2 tsp vanilla extract

6 eggs

1 tsp grated lemon rind

1 tbsp lemon juice

1 cup seedless raisins

4 cups cooked rice

1 cup graham cracker crumbs

In a large mixing bowl, beat together the milk, salt, sugar, butter, vanilla and eggs. Stir in the lemon rind, lemon juice and raisins. Add the cooked rice and mix well.

Preheat oven to 325°F. Butter a large baking dish, and coat the bottom and sides with graham cracker crumbs.

Pour the pudding into the dish and bake for 1 hour and 10 minutes.

Serve hot, or allow to cool down to room temperature, then refrigerate until serving time. Serve plain or with a bottled fruit syrup such as boysenberry or raspberry syrup.

ONE OF THE LOVELIEST Christmas decorations is the poinsettia. This plant has tiny flowers surrounded by large flower-like upper leaves which turn brilliant red (or less commonly, pink or white) in the winter months. With the striking contrast between the red and green leaves, the poinsettia rivals the holly as one of the most popular Christmas plants.

The poinsettia is native to Mexico, and was first brought to America in 1828 by Joel Roberts Poinsett, a botanist and the first American ambassador to Mexico. By the early 1830's, the poinsettias were being grown in Charleston, North Carolina (Poinsett's home), and by other botanist friends in Philadelphia. By the early 1900s, flower growers in California had developed the potted Christmas poinsettia.

A lovely legend from Mexico tells of Pablo, a poor young Mexican boy who picked a branch of the plant to bring to Jesus at the shrine of the nativity. When Pablo placed the plant at the alter, the leaves miraculously turned brilliant red and his gift was transformed into a beautiful flower.

My son-in-law, Bruce, usually brings a poinsettia plant for Marg and me in late November. As well, many friends, knowing our love for these plants, also send one or two to each of us. By Christmas, our home begins to resemble a flower shop, and that is just the way we love it.

SOMETIME DURING THE holiday, Bruce and Marg host a group of Bruce's co-workers at an open house cocktail party. Marg and I enjoy making a number of hot and cold hors d'oeuvres.

Many of my favourite hors d'oeuvres are made with seafood—no doubt a bit of my east coast upbringing showing through. Here are two different ways to serve lobster.

Lobster Bites

1 package frozen east coast (or South African) lobster tails

1 tbsp mixed pickling spices

1 slice of onion

1/2 tsp salt

Lemon juice

Bottled cocktail sauce or tartar sauce

Cook the lobster tails with pickling spices, onion and salt, following label directions on the spices. Drain and cool completely.

With scissors, cut through and remove the thick membrane on the underside of the lobster shell. Take out the lobster meat by peeling the hard shell back with one hand and pulling the meat toward you with the other. Cut the meat into 1/2-inch slices. Sprinkle with lemon juice, cover and chill.

Serve with a dip of cocktail sauce, tartar sauce or with lemon wedges to squeeze.

Lobster Baskets

These look wonderful on any hors d'oeuvres tray.

1 loaf unsliced, firm white bread

4 tbsp melted butter or margarine

1 can (5 oz.) lobster meat

1 pimento

3 tablespoons mayonnaise

2 tsp lemon juice

Trim end crusts from bread. Cut the loaf crosswise into 6 1-inch slices. Trim slices to 3-inch squares. With a sharp tip knife, hollow out the squares to make tiny baskets. Brush with melted butter and place on a cookie sheet.

Bake bread slices at 350°F for 12 minutes or until golden. Remove from the oven and set aside to cool.

Drain lobster and pimento and finely chop both. Mix with mayonnaise and lemon juice in a small bowl. About an hour before serving, spoon the lobster mixture into the bread baskets, using about 1 teaspoonful for each. Garnish with bits of cucumber or bits of lemon if you wish.

MY SON-IN-LAW JOHN LOVES scallops and this next recipe is one of his favourites.

Petites coquilles St-Jacques

1/2 pound fresh sea scallops (or frozen scallops, thawed)

2 tbsp milk

3 tbsp flour

4 tbsp butter or margarine

2 tsp lemon juice

1 tbsp minced parsley

Cup scallops into tiny cubes and place in medium sized bowl. Sprinkle milk over the top, then flour. Toss to coat well.

Heat 2 tbsp of the butter in a medium sized frying pan; add scallops, tossing to coat well with butter. Cook just 3 minutes or until lightly browned; remove from heat. Stir in lemon juice and parsley.

Heat remaining 2 tbsp butter slowly until golden brown in a small frying pan; pour over scallops.

When ready to serve, spoon the scallop mixture into tiny scallop shells. Serve hot.

Makes 18 servings

STAYING WITH OUR SEAFOOD theme, the next two recipes feature clams and shrimps.

Little Clambakes

8 ounces light cream cheese, softened

1 8-ounce can minced clams, drained

1 tbsp bottled onion juice
1/2 tsp liquid red pepper seasoning
4 dozen crackers
Paprika
Olives and watercress for garnish (optional)

In a medium sized bowl, combine softened cream cheese, clams, onion juice and red pepper seasoning. Mix well to blend. (If made ahead, cover and store in refrigerator.)

Just before serving, preheat the oven to 400°F. Spread the clam mixture on crackers, about 1 teaspoonful on each. Sprinkle lightly with paprika and place on large cookie sheets. Bake for 5 minutes or until just heated, but not browned. Garnish with olives and watercress if desired.

Makes 4 dozen

Shrimp Newburg Tarts

3 dozen tiny frozen tartlet shells
2 tins (12 ounces) cocktail shrimp, drained
4 tbsp butter or margarine
1 tbsp flour
1/2 tsp salt
1/4 tsp pepper
Dash of ground nutmeg
1 cup light cream or table cream
1 egg yolk
2 tbsp dry sherry

Prick the bottoms of the tartlet shells and bake according to package directions. Cool completely.

Set aside 36 small shrimp for garnish. Place remainder of shrimp in tartlet shells. Set shells in a large shallow baking pan.

Melt butter in a small saucepan. Stir in flour, salt, pepper, and nutmeg. Cook, stirring constantly until bubbly. Stir in cream and continue cooking until the sauce thickens and boils for 1 minute.

Beat egg yolk in a small bowl. Beat in about half of the hot sauce, then stir the egg-yolk mixture back into remaining sauce in the pan. Cook, stirring constantly, for 1 minute. Stir in sherry. Spoon over shrimps in shells.

Bake in 300°F oven for 15 minutes, or until hot. Garnish with reserved shrimps. Serve hot…and wait for the raves. It seems that everyone loves these little tarts.

DIFFICULT AS IT IS to imagine, some people don't like seafood. For those poor misguided souls, Marg and I make other finger foods to enjoy.

Rumaki

12 chicken livers, halved at the natural separation

24 thin slivers of water chestnut

12 slices of bacon, cut in half

1 1/2 cups soy sauce

1 clove garlic, minced

1 cup light brown sugar

Make a small incision in the centre of each chicken liver half and insert a sliver of water chestnut. Wrap each piece of liver with a half slice of bacon and hold in place with a toothpick.

Mix soy sauce and garlic, add chicken livers, cover and marinate in the refrigerator for several hours.

Just before serving, remove livers from the marinade, roll lightly in brown sugar and broil until bacon is crisp. Serve hot.

Party Pork Balls

1 pound ground pork

1 8-ounce can water chestnuts, minced

1/2 cup minced green onions

1 tsp minced fresh or preserved ginger

3/4 tsp salt

1 tbsp soy sauce

1 egg, lightly beaten

1/2 cup packaged bread crumbs

Cornstarch

3 tsp vegetable oil

Sweet and sour sauce (recipe follows)

Combine pork, water chestnuts, onions, ginger, salt, soy sauce, egg and bread crumbs in a large bowl; mix well. Shape into 36 balls. Roll each ball in cornstarch to coat lightly, shaking off excess. Brown the meatballs in oil in a large skillet. Remove them as they brown to a roasting pan and cover loosely with foil.

Bake in a pre-heated 350°F oven for 20 minutes or until thoroughly cooked. Combine with sweet and sour sauce and serve in a chafing dish with decorative tooth-picks.

Sweet and Sour Sauce

1/2 cup sweet green pepper, cubed

1/2 cup sweet red pepper, cubed

2 large carrots, thinly sliced

2 tbsp vegetable oil

1 20-ounce can pineapple chunks with juice

1/4 cup vinegar

1 tbsp soy sauce

2 tbsp sugar

1/2 cup beef broth

2 tsp minced fresh ginger

2 tbsp corn starch

1/3 cup water

In a large saucepan, sauté the green pepper, red pepper and carrots in vegetable oil for about 3 minutes or until tender. Stir in the pineapple chunks and the juice, vinegar, soy sauce, sugar, broth and ginger.

Combine cornstarch and water in a cup then stir into the sauce. Cook, stirring constantly, until the mixture thickens.

Marg always serves a variety of vegetables and dips as well as the hot hors d'oeuvres so that even folks who may be on a restricted diet may enjoy a little something.

FOR MANY OF US who are senior citizens living on a fixed income, finding inexpensive appropriate Christmas gifts can sometimes be a difficult task.

My dear friend Alice solved her problem in a way that I think is wonderful. She explained, "You know Edna, when James and I were married we were very fortunate. We both came from families that were well to do and over the years we were given many rather extravagant gifts. We had several sets of elegant china, crystal and silver, dozens of silver or crystal serving dishes as well as silver candle holders, and a collection of Royal Doulton figurines.

"A few years ago, I decided to give some of these things to my family while I am alive, instead of leaving them in my will. I don't have an enormous income, but I do have lovely things that I rarely use. I decided that I would much rather see them used by my children or grandchildren when I can enjoy the pleasure that these gifts bring to them."

Often a gift takes more ingenuity than money. My friend and neighbour Lila MacGuinness usually has some wonderful ideas for gifts, as well. This year Lila decided to give each person a Christmas decoration that she made. She purchased a number of votive candles in small glasses, and decorated them with a variety of dried materials. For example, using a hot glue gun, she attached dried bay leaves to the sides of the glass. A red candle decorated with a raffia bow and a cluster of holly berries would be welcomed in any home.

Lila also decorates votive candles with cinnamon sticks or twigs glued vertically around the side. A raffia bow and a cluster of berries or a rose hip completes the gift.

After an afternoon of making gifts, writing cards, or decorating the house, Lila and I enjoy a quiet evening dinner together. We turn on the Christmas music, light candles, and reminisce about Christmas long ago. It really is a lovely time for both of us.

Our dinner is usually a bit of work, but I thought perhaps you might enjoy something special when there are just two of you.

Consommé with Barley

2 cups beef consommé or homemade beef broth

1/4 cup peeled and thinly sliced carrots

2 dried European mushrooms

1/2 cup barley

1/2 tsp salt

1/4 tsp pepper

2 slices lemon for garnish (optional)

Soak the barley in cold water overnight. Pour about 1/2 cup boiling water over the dried mushrooms in a bowl and soak for two hours. Reserve the liquid.

Bring the consommé to a simmer in a saucepan over medium low heat. Add the carrots, salt and pepper and simmer 5 minutes.

Remove mushrooms from their liquid and chop finely, then add to the saucepan. Strain the mushroom liquid through a piece of cheesecloth and add it to the soup. Drain the barley and add to the soup. Cover and simmer over low heat for 20 minutes. Serve hot, garnished with a slice of lemon, if desired.

ALTHOUGH LILA AND I don't always finish our Rock Cornish hens, they make a nice lunch the next day.

Rock Cornish Hens with Wild Rice Stuffing

Wild Rice Stuffing:

2 tbsp chopped shallots

1/2 tsp salt

1 cup chicken broth

2 tbsp butter

1/2 cup wild rice

Preheat oven to 350°F. In a saucepan, melt the butter and simmer the chopped shallots in it until they soften. Add the chicken broth, salt and wild rice. Stir well, cover, and simmer over low heat for about 15 minutes until the rice has absorbed the liquid. Remove from the heat and set aside.

Hens:

2 Cornish hens, completely thawed

2 tbsp butter

1/2 tsp salt

1/4 tsp poultry seasoning

1/4 tsp pepper

1 cup chicken broth

2 strips bacon, cut in half

Dry the inside of the hens with a paper towel and season the cavities with salt and pepper. Stuff the hens with Wild Rice Stuffing and truss.

Butter the outside of the hens, sprinkle with poultry seasoning, and arrange the strips of bacon over the breasts. Place the hens on a rack in a roasting pan.

Roast for 45 minutes, basting frequently with drippings; add some of the chicken broth if needed. When the hens are done, remove from the roasting pan. Add the chicken broth to the pan, place on a burner, and bring to a boil. Scrape all the drippings into the boiling broth to make the gravy.

To serve, partially cut the legs and the thighs away from the bodies of the hens and break through the wing joints. Serve immediately with the hot gravy.

ALTHOUGH I DON'T ALWAYS do potatoes with this dinner—I find the rice stuffing quite sufficient—some people don't feel a dinner is complete without them. For you, I offer steamed buttered potatoes.

Steamed Buttered Potatoes

2 large potatoes

1 tbsp butter

1 tsp chopped parsley

1 tsp salt

Steam the potatoes on a rack over boiling water for at least 20 minutes, or until they are cooked through. (It may be necessary to add water to avoid burning the pot.)

Remove potatoes to a serving dish. Add the butter, salt and parsley, and toss until the butter is almost melted and the parsley adheres to the potatoes. Serve hot.

ASPARAGUS IS ONE OF my favourite vegetables, and this is one of my favourite ways to serve it. Most large supermarkets seem to carry asparagus year round, but in desperation, frozen asparagus will do.

Hot Asparagus Tips with Crumbled Bacon

4 strips lean bacon

1 bunch fresh asparagus (12–16 pieces)

2 tbsp melted butter

Tie the asparagus together with a string and stand the bunch up on the thick ends; untie only after cooking. Steam the asparagus in a very deep pot, for about 15 minutes in about 3 inches of water.

While the asparagus is steaming, fry the bacon until it is crisp. Drain it on a piece of towel, then crumble it into a small bowl.

When the steaming is done, remove the asparagus from the pot and cut off about 4 inches from the thick ends.

Divide the asparagus into 2 portions. Put the butter on the tips and sprinkle with the crumbled bacon. Serve hot.

FOR OUR DESSERT, YOU NEED either two 1-cup individual molds, or one 2-cup mold.

Coconut Gelatin with Raspberry Sauce

1 cup milk

1 cup cream of coconut concentrate (available canned)

5 drops almond extract

1 envelope unflavoured gelatin

4 tbsp sugar

1 tbsp brandy

1 package frozen raspberries

Dissolve the gelatin in the milk, stirring until all the grains are absorbed. Place the milk in a heavy saucepan and stir in the coconut concentrate. Heat almost to the boiling point, but do not allow to boil. Stir in the almond extract, sugar and brandy, and warm another 2 minutes to melt the sugar. Remove from the heat.

Pour the mixture into the mold(s) and refrigerate for several hours until the gelatin is set. While the gelatin is setting, thaw the frozen raspberries.

To serve, un-mold the gelatin onto a serving plate or two individual dessert plates. Spoon over thawed raspberries and serve.

O Christmas Tree, O Christmas tree
You come from God, eternal.
A symbol of the Lord of Love
Whom God to man sent from above.
O Christmas tree, O Christmas tree,
You come from God, eternal.

traditional German carol

AMONG THE SYMBOLS OF Christmas, the tree is one of the most important. Long before the tree became a part of Christmas, evergreens were closely associated with pagan ceremonies. Trees were decorated during the ancient Roman festival of Saturnalia. In Northern Europe, Druids honoured their gods by tying tributes to tree branches. With the advent of Christianity and the teachings of early Christian missionaries, evergreens began to lose their association with pagan rituals. The tree became a universal symbol of Christianity—the tree of the Christ child who brought new life to the world.

We thank St. Boniface for this. St. Boniface, an 8th-century missionary among the heathen tribes of Germany, cut down the sacred oak of Odin. Behind it stood a small fir tree which he dedicated to the infant Jesus. About 800 years later, Martin Luther decorated a fir tree with candles for his children. By the late 18th century, evergreen Christmas trees were popular in Germany.

The Christmas tree with its candles gleaming
A glow is kindling in all our hearts,
It speaks of God's pure love-light streaming;
It brings us hope and joy imparts.

traditional German carol

When Prince Albert, consort to Queen Victoria, imported fir trees from his native Coburg and set them up at Windsor castle, the English gentry quickly approved of the custom. In an 1848 edition of the *Illustrated London News*, the royal family is shown gathered around their tree. From that time on, decorated trees were a part of Christmas celebrations in England. The custom spread quickly to North America, and in 1882 the first American Christmas tree lit with electric lights, thrilled the people of New York City.

Although artificial Christmas trees enjoyed popularity in the 1970s, the evergreen has returned to its number one ranking once again.

IN OUR FAMILY, WE have made tree selecting an art form. We march off into the woods not to be seen again until the perfect tree has been found. Because of the time involved in the selection process, we often take along a hamper of food. I'm not quite sure what the tree farm owner thinks when he sees all of us head off carting picnic baskets, but the look of relief on his face when we return is quite comical.

Actually, a winter picnic is quite enjoyable. If you aren't sure what to take with you, perhaps these next recipes will give you some ideas.

We always bring along a hearty soup, and Philadelphia Pepper Pot certainly fills the bill. A large thermos is perfect to keep the soup hot while en route.

Philadelphia Pepper Pot

4 slices bacon

1 medium onion, minced

1 stalk celery with leaves, minced

1 small green pepper, minced

3/4 pound honeycomb tripe, diced

8 cups chicken broth

1 bay leaf

1/2 tsp pepper

Salt to taste

1 cup diced raw potato

3 tbsp butter

3 tbsp flour

1/2 cup light cream

Dice the bacon and sauté in a heavy saucepan. Add the onion, celery and green pepper and simmer for 10 minutes. Add the tripe, broth, bay leaf, pepper and salt to the bacon mixture and bring to a boil. Add the potato, cover and simmer for 1 1/2 hours.

Melt the butter, blend in the flour and a little of the soup liquid, then add to the hot soup and bring to a boil. Season with more salt and pepper (to taste), and just before serving, stir in the cream.

Serves 6–8

ROSEMARY SCONES GO WELL with this soup, and are quite easily made.

Rosemary Scones

1/3 cup buttermilk, plus extra for brushing

1 large egg

1 tsp minced fresh rosemary

1 tsp coarse salt

1/2 tsp grated lemon zest

2 1/4 cups unsifted all-purpose flour

2 tsp baking powder

1/4 tsp baking soda

1/2 cup cold, unsalted butter, cut into bits

Preheat oven to 400°F. In a small bowl, whisk together the buttermilk, egg, 1/4 tsp each of rosemary and salt, and the lemon zest.

In a large bowl, combine flour, baking powder and baking soda. With a pastry blender or 2 knives used in scissor fashion, cut the butter into the flour mixture until the mixture resembles coarse meal. With fork, stir in the buttermilk mixture just until blended; do not over-mix. Press dough together into a ball.

On a lightly floured service, roll out the dough into an 8-inch round. Cut the round into 12 equal-size wedges. Brush the top of each wedge with buttermilk and sprinkle with the remaining rosemary and salt. Place wedges on a baking sheet. Bake for 13–15 minutes, or until the tops of the scones are lightly browned.

Serve with wedges of cheddar cheese—scrumptious!

BAKED BEANS AND WIENERS are also popular picnic items. To make good baked beans, you must have a bean-pot. We are lucky to have several pots of varying sizes; for 6–8 servings I use a medium pot.

Vermont Baked Beans

1 pound yellow eye or pea beans
1/2 tsp baking soda
1 tsp salt
1/3 cup maple syrup

1/2 tsp dry mustard

1 small onion, whole but peeled

1/2 pound salt pork

Put beans in a beanpot, cover with cold water, and let stand overnight. In the morning, drain, cover with fresh water and add the soda. Cover and simmer until beans are just tender. Do not overcook! (A good test is to spoon out a bean or two and blow on them; if the skin cracks, the beans are ready.) Drain the beans. Add salt, maple syrup and mustard. Tuck the peeled whole onion well down in the centre of the pot. Add boiling water just to the top of the beans. Score the salt pork and place it on the surface.

Cover the pot and bake at 275°F for at least 4 hours. You can rarely bake beans too long, so don't worry about them. However, good baked beans should never be dry; inspect them occasionally and add a bit of boiling water if necessary.

We actually take the bean pot with us, wrapped in towels or blankets. The pot stays hot and so do the beans. We also take wieners in hot water in a thermos so that they stay hot and don't dry out.

HOT DRINKS ARE ALWAYS welcome on a winter picnic. Hot Tea Nectar is a different but delectable drink to take with you. This recipe makes 30 servings. You might leave half behind and reheat it when you arrive home.

Hot Tea Nectar

8 cups boiling water

8 regular size tea bags

1 can (18 ounces) unsweetened pineapple juice

1 can (18 ounces) apricot nectar

1 can (6 ounces) frozen lemon juice

1 can (6 ounces) frozen orange juice concentrate

1 cup sugar

2 1/4 cups water

Pour boiling water over tea bags in a large kettle or pot. Cover, steep for 5 minutes, then remove tea bags.

Combine pineapple juice, apricot nectar, lemon juice, orange concentrate, sugar and water in a large pot. Heat slowly, stirring several times, to simmering. Stir in hot tea.

Pour into a thermos to keep hot. When you arrive home, re-heat in the large pot and add slices of lemon and lime before ladling into mugs.

ONCE YOU HAVE THE tree at home, it is time to fumble about in the basement looking for the boxes of lights and decorations. In some homes, where there is an organized mother, you hear the words "second shelf on the left, third and fourth boxes from the right, dear." In many others, like ours, the intentions were good but I believe they paved a road...well, you know the rest. I do confess that I love the conversation, though.

"Where are the boxes of decorations, Marg?"

"Why they're in the basement, wherever you put them away last year, dear."

"Well the light-bulb just burned out. Do you have another?"

"Actually no, but the flashlight is just at the top of the stairs."

"This flashlight is quite dim, Marg."

"Well it won't matter. I'm sure you'll remember exactly where you put them, dear. Remember the box doesn't say 'Decorations,' it says 'Jenny's bedroom' because it was an old box from when Phyllis moved."

"Ouch, d—-!"

"Something wrong, dear?"

"Why is the hockey net in the middle of the cupboard?"

"I think you left it there after you played with Justin, dear."

" I give up Marg! Let's just buy new ones."

"Oh, Bruce, don't be silly. Look, here they are, right in front of you."

This ritual happens each year, and I laugh every time.

THERE IS NOTHING WE enjoy more than a tree decorating party. It's fun to have family and friends over to string the lights and hang the balls, other heirloom toys and tinsel. This can be a hunger-inducing job, and it seems that everyone loves to eat pizza when that last ornament has been hung. My grandson Marshall is the king of the pizza makers in our family. I hope you'll enjoy it as much as we do.

Marshall's Magnificent Pizza

First make the dough:

2 cups warm (not hot) water

2 packages active dry yeast

2 tsp sugar

2 tsp salt

1/4 cup olive oil

7 cups sifted flour

Measure water into a bowl and sprinkle with yeast. Stir until dissolved. Stir in sugar, salt and olive oil. Add four cups of the flour, beat until smooth, then add as much of the remaining flour as is needed to make a dough. Turn out on a floured board and knead until smooth and elastic. Place in a large greased bowl, then invert the dough so it is greased all over. Cover and let rise in a warm place, free from drafts, until doubled in bulk (about 45 minutes).

Now the sauce and toppings:

1 1/3 cups (2 6-ounce cans) tomato paste

1 cup water

2 tsp salt

2 tsp crushed oregano

1/4 tsp pepper

1 pound mozzarella cheese, grated

1/2 cup olive oil

1/2 cup grated Parmesan or Romano cheese

A selection of any or all of the following: sliced pepperoni, chopped onions, sliced green or black olives, sliced ham, pineapple chunks, sliced green, red or yellow pepper, mushrooms, chopped fresh tomatoes. For a change, you might also try strips of grilled chicken breast, broccoli and sun-dried tomatoes. Feta cheese also adds a new flavour.

The dough and the sauce recipes will make four 12-inch round pizzas. Two or three people might like to decorate one pizza to their liking. You get an interesting variety this way.

Mix together the tomato paste, water, salt, oregano, and pepper. Get the remaining ingredients ready and preheat the oven to 400°F.

When the dough has risen, punch down by pushing your fist into the dough. Turn out on a board. Divide into quarters. Form each into a ball and place on greased baking sheets or twelve-inch pizza pans. Press and gently pull with fingers into circles twelve inches in diameter. The dough should be quite thin, with edges about 1/4-inch thick.

On each circle of dough, arrange one quarter of the tomato mixture, 2 tbsp olive oil, 2 tbsp grated Romano or Parmesan cheese, selected toppings and one quarter of the shredded mozzarella cheese.

Bake for 25 minutes or until the cheese is hot and bubbly.

Makes 4 pizzas

THE FIRST YEAR THAT George and I were married, we were in a new parish, George's first, and rather short of funds for luxuries such as tree decorations. We chopped down our tree on a Friday evening and George managed to make an acceptable wooden holder to keep it upright. I can only assume that someone passed the word that the new pastor and his wife had been seen trailing home their tree, for on Saturday morning, and indeed all day long, parishioners came by our home to introduce themselves and drop off decorations for our tree. It seemed as if each one wanted to give us their loveliest decorative heirlooms. By Saturday evening we had a Christmas tree that was lovely beyond our wildest dreams. It was a marvelous way to make us feel welcome!

George and I treasured those decorations. Whenever we moved, which we did quite often, a little bit of our east coast home went with us. Over the years, I have given a number of these treasures to members of my family. I feel such joy when I visit their homes during the holidays and see that our decorations of so long ago have a place of honour on their tree.

SOME SUNDAY MORNING after church we like to have a brunch for our neighbours. At this time of year it's nice to let people know how much you appreciate their kindness over the past year and a brunch seems an enjoyable way to do just that.

My dear friend Elaine in Shelburne was happy to pass along two of her favourite brunch recipes for us to use. They are especially nice as they can be prepared ahead of time. This allows you to visit with your guests instead of working in the kitchen.

Savoury Baked Sandwiches

8 slices bread, crust removed

Slices of ham

Sharp cheddar cheese

3 eggs

2 cups milk

1 1/4 tsp salt

The night before your brunch, place 4 slices of bread in a flat pan. Cover each slice first with ham then with cheese. Top with remaining bread slices.

In a bowl, mix eggs, milk and salt. Beat and pour over the sandwiches. Let stand overnight, then bake at 350°F for one hour.

Serve with curried fruit.

Serves 4

Curried Fruit

1 small can peaches,

1 small can pears

1 small can pineapple rings

Several maraschino cherries

1/2 cup melted butter

1/2 cup brown sugar

2 tbsp corn starch

2 tsp curry powder

In a casserole, combine the fruit. Mix together the remaining ingredients in a bowl. Pour over the fruit and bake (together with the sandwiches above) for one hour at 350°F.

Serves 4

MY SON-IN-LAW JOHN particularly enjoys French toast. We make him responsible for this part of our brunch, a job he enjoys very much. People always come back for seconds. The secret probably is in the deliciously different sauce.

John's Favourite French Toast

12 3/4-inch thick slices French bread

3 tbsp unsalted butter

Batter:

6 large eggs

1 1/2 cups heavy cream

1 1/2 tbsp vanilla extract

2 tsp cinnamon

3/4 tsp fresh grated nutmeg

Sauce:

2 cups maple syrup

1 cup honey

1 tbsp vanilla

1 cup sliced almonds, lightly toasted

*1 cup dried mixed fruits, such as cherries, apples, apricots,
    peaches and raisins.*

Make the sauce first. In a saucepan warm maple syrup, honey and vanilla over medium-low heat, stirring. Add nuts and dried fruits. Bring mixture just to a boil and remove the pan from the heat.

To make the batter, whisk all ingredients together in a large bowl until they are well blended.

In a large non-stick pan, heat 1 tbsp butter over moderate heat until foam subsides. Dip bread slices into batter and let the excess drip off. Cook in batches until golden and crisp, about 2 minutes on each side, adding remaining butter to the pan as needed. Transfer the toast, as cooked, to paper towels to drain.

Serve French toast warm with sauce and fresh fruit to garnish.

Serves 6

Fruit juices and coffee, along with a variety of cookies and squares, complete a brunch that all will enjoy.

A VICTORIAN CHRISTMAS CELEBRATION was never complete without games. One strange game called Snapdragon was very popular. A dish of brandy was placed on the floor and set aflame. Handfuls of currants were tossed into the bowl and the object of the game was to grab a burning currant out of the fire—in your mouth—and in doing so extinguish it.

Happily many other games were far less dangerous; Hide and Seek, Bob Apple, and Blind Man's Bluff are familiar still today. Charades was also a popular pastime.

Pantomime theatre performances, also a Victorian favourite, are often performed here in Canada. I can remember going to the Royal Alexandra theatre in Toronto for a Boxing Day performance.

Our family particularly enjoys *The Nutcracker,* a ballet performed annually by the National Ballet of Canada. Even the young boys in the family will grudgingly admit to having enjoyed the performance.

After-theatre snacks are just the ticket, but it's nice to have something light so as not to go to sleep on an excruciatingly full stomach. A slice of angel food cake is light, delicious, and has no fat. What a great way to end an evening.

Cappuccino Angel Food Cake

1 cup cake flour (not self-rising)

1/2 cup plus 1 tbsp confectioners' sugar

1 2/3 cups egg whites (about 1 dozen large eggs)

4 tsp instant espresso powder

1 1/2 tsp cream of tartar

1/2 tsp salt

1/2 plus 1/8 tsp ground cinnamon

1 1/2 tsp vanilla extract

1 1/4 cups granulated sugar

Preheat oven to 375°F. On waxed paper, mix flour and 1/2 cup confectioners' sugar. Set aside.

In a large bowl, with mixer at high speed, beat egg whites with instant espresso, cream of tartar, salt and 1/2 tsp cinnamon until soft peaks form. Beat in vanilla. Beating at high speed, sprinkle in granulated sugar, 2 tbsp at a time; beat until the sugar completely dissolves and the egg whites stand in stiff, glossy peaks.

Sift flour mixture over egg whites, one third at a time, and fold in with a rubber spatula after each addition, just until the flour disappears.

Spoon batter into an ungreased 10-inch tube pan. Bake 35 to 40 minutes, until the top springs back when lightly touched.

Invert the cake pan on a funnel or a bottle. Cool completely in the pan. (If removed from the pan too early, the cake will lose volume and collapse.)

With a metal spatula, carefully loosen the cake from the pan; place on a cake plate. In a cup, mix remaining confectioners' sugar and cinnamon and sprinkle over the top of the cake.

Served with a hot cup of tea or coffee, it is the perfect ending to a night at the theatre.

O little town of Bethlehem,
How still we see thee lie!
Above thy deep and dreamless sleep
The silent stars go by;
Yet in thy dark streets shineth
The everlasting light;
The hopes and fears of all the years
Are met in thee tonight.

Philip Brooks

CHRISTMAS EVE IS A night of delightful celebrations. It is a time for visitors; friends, relatives and neighbours come to share the wonderful warm spirit of this special night. Children hang their stockings and then rush to bed, where they listen intently for the tinkle of sleigh bells or the sounds of reindeer hooves on the roof that signal Santa's arrival.

For us, it is a time to spend with family. As many family members as possible come together to celebrate Christmas. Usually, by Christmas Eve, everyone has arrived. It is a time for last minute gift wrapping, catching up on all the news since our last gathering, and enjoying each other's company.

This meal was always George's responsibility. He loved making traditional, east coast chowder, and this recipe came from his mother. After his passing, my son-in-law Bruce took over the chowder and I know how happy George would be to know that Bruce has mastered this family culinary delight.

Salt Cod Chowder

1 pound salt codfish

6 slices of salt pork, 1/4-inch thick, diced

8 medium potatoes, peeled and diced

4 medium onions, peeled and diced

10 cups milk

2 cups cream

Salt and pepper to taste

Flake the codfish and soak in lukewarm water until the fish is soft and the salt has been removed. Drain and discard the water.

Fry the salt pork in a large heavy saucepan. When golden brown, add potatoes, onions and codfish. Simmer gently in as little water as possible for about 20 minutes or until the fish and vegetables are tender. Add the milk, cream and salt and pepper to taste, and heat until hot but not boiling. Transfer to a large, warmed, soup tureen.

Serves 10–12

Almost any type of biscuits or rolls may be served with this chowder, but 60-minute-rolls are fast and delicious.

60-Minute Rolls

2 packages active dry yeast

1/3 cup warm water

1 1/4 cups milk

2 tbsp shortening

3 tbsp sugar

1 tsp salt

3 1/2 cups flour

Dissolve the yeast in warm water. Heat the milk. Add the shortening, sugar, salt, and egg, allow the mixture to cool, and add the yeast. Add the flour and beat well; the dough will be sticky. Set dough in a warm place and let it rise for 15 minutes.

Punch the dough down and knead lightly. Roll out the dough to 3/4 inch thickness and use a round cookie cutter to make the rolls. Place rolls about 1 inch apart on a lightly greased cookie sheet. Let rise 15 minutes and bake at 400°F for 15 minutes.

Makes 15 rolls

Serve with wedges of cheese, vegetables and dip and the family will be ready for anything that Christmas Eve brings.

SANTA CLAUS, "CHUBBY AND plump—a right jolly old elf" is a traditional part of Christmas folklore. The origin of Santa Claus can be traced back to St. Nicholas, a generous bishop in fourth-century Turkey who was said to perform kind deeds and bring gifts to the needy. Over time St. Nicholas evolved into a magical figure who could fly (as witches did), and use chimneys as doors (like the Norse gods).

Santa's physical image has changed over the years. For hundreds of years St. Nicholas was imagined to be tall and thin. However, in "A Visit from St. Nicholas," a poem written in 1822 by Clement C. Moore, the saint is pictured as a round figure wearing fur and riding in a sleigh pulled by eight reindeer.

An 1863 drawing by American political cartoonist Thomas Nast depicts Santa Claus as a big, red-faced, white-bearded, jolly man wearing sprigs of mistletoe and holly on his hat. Thomas Nast's famous 1866 drawing, "Santa Claus and his Works" showing Santa in his workshop with a record of the good and bad deeds of all children, appeared as a Christmas picture in *Harper's Weekly*.

IT IS COMMON FOR CHILDREN to leave a special snack for Santa and fruits or vegetables for his reindeer. This year Santa Claus may enjoy his choice of a Sour Cream Peach Muffin or a Cranberry Muffin.

Sour Cream Peach Muffins

1 1/2 cups brown sugar, firmly packed

2/3 cup light vegetable oil

1 egg

1 cup sour cream

1 tsp baking soda

1 tsp vanilla extract

1 tsp salt

2 1/4 cups flour

1 1/2 cups peaches (fresh or canned)

1/2 cup chopped nuts (optional)

Butter and cinnamon sugar (for tops)

Preheat the oven to 325°F. Combine the sugar, oil and egg in a mixing bowl. In another bowl, combine the sour cream, salt, vanilla and soda. Add the sour cream mixture to the sugar mixture and slowly blend in the flour. Do not over mix. Fold in the peaches (and nuts if using).

Pour the batter into muffin cups, sprinkle the tops with cinnamon sugar, and put a bit of butter on top of each muffin. Bake for 30 minutes.

Makes 12 to 15 muffins

Cranberry Muffins

1 or 2 oranges

2 cups all-purpose flour

1 tbsp baking powder

2/3 cup plus 1 tsp granulated sugar

1 cup coarsely chopped cranberries

1 cup chopped walnuts

1/3 cup melted butter or safflower oil

1 egg

Preheat the oven to 400°F. Grease a muffin pan or line with paper cups. Remove the zest from the oranges, mince and measure out 1 tbsp and 1 tsp. Squeeze the juice and reserve 2/3 cup.

In a large bowl, combine flour, baking powder, and 2/3 cup sugar. In a medium bowl toss together cranberries, nuts, and orange zest. In another medium bowl, combine orange juice, melted butter and egg. Whisk until blended. Pour the liquid over the flour mixture and stir three to four times to combine. Add the cranberry nut mixture and combine using as few strokes as possible. (The batter should be lumpy.) Pour in to muffin cups. Sprinkle a pinch of the remaining sugar over each muffin. Bake on the middle rack of the oven for 25 minutes or until golden brown. Let cool on a wire rack for 15–20 minutes.

Makes 12–15 muffins

CHRISTMAS EVE IS ALSO the time that we usually set the dining table for Christmas dinner. If ever there is a time to use your best china, crystal, and silver, this is it. Even if you have none of those things, you can make the table special in many other ways. Napkins or place mats made from inexpensive cotton Christmas material will look great against a plain white tablecloth. Fresh flowers combined with pine boughs, pinecones, and berries and holly can make any table look festive. Add as many candles as will fit and you will have a beautiful table that will make the meal memorable.

When we were young there were too many of us to fit at one table. I remember that Grandma would set the large

dining room table for the adults and a smaller table for all of the children in the family. Your chance of moving to the big table, even as you outgrew the children's table, usually depended on one of the adults being absent (or having passed away). The first year of sitting at the adult table was eagerly anticipated.

Wherever you sat, the Christmas cracker was, and still is, essential. Tom Smith, a Victorian confectioner's apprentice, invented this popular Christmas favour—a paper cylinder containing a message of endearment, small candies and a saltpetre friction strip to add the bang when it is pulled open. Today's crackers contain a rhyme, a paper hat and a small gift, and they still bang when opened. The more expensive the cracker, the better the gift.

Sometimes, while setting the tables, I like to put out some small snacks. They serve two purposes: they help keep people from being too hungry before tomorrow's breakfast, and they give those of us setting the table the chance to do so without too many people underfoot.

Cheddar Cheese Balls

1 1/2 cups sharp cheddar cheese, shredded

8 ounces cream cheese, softened

1 tsp minced garlic

1 tsp Worcestershire sauce

1 tbsp dried parsley flakes

3/4 cup finely chopped walnuts

Spread the walnuts on a cookie sheet with sides. Combine all ingredients, except the nuts, in a medium sized bowl, and blend well. Divide into 3 or 4 balls of equal size. Roll the balls in the walnuts until they are well coated. Leave them on the cookie sheet, covered with plastic wrap and refrigerate until serving.

To serve, put the balls on individual plates and surround with a variety of crackers.

THIS CLAM DIP MAY be served with raw vegetables or with taco chips.

Clam Dip

8 ounces creamed cottage cheese

4 ounces cream cheese

2 tsp prepared horseradish

1 tsp Worcestershire sauce

1 can (about 10 1/2 ounces) minced clams, drained

3–4 tbsp light cream or table cream

Paprika

Blend cottage cheese, cream cheese, horseradish and Worcestershire sauce in a medium bowl. Stir in the clams; chill. When ready to serve, beat in enough cream to thin the mixture for dipping. Spoon into small bowls and sprinkle with paprika.

THESE MUSHROOMS ARE A delicious treat anytime, and
they also look elegant enough to be served at a party.

Hot Stuffed Mushrooms

1/2 cup unsalted butter

1/3 cup green pepper, minced

1/3 cup red bell peppers, minced

1/4 cup onion, minced

2 cloves garlic, minced

1/8 tsp cayenne

1 egg, beaten

1/4 cup freshly grated parmesan cheese

1/3 cup crabmeat

1/2 cup breadcrumbs

24 firm white mushrooms, stems removed

Sauté peppers, onions and garlic in 1/4 cup butter until they
are soft. Remove from heat and add egg, cheese, crabmeat
and breadcrumbs.

Melt the remaining 1/4 cup butter. Dip each cap in
melted butter and stuff with the crabmeat mixture. Bake at
400°F until lightly browned on top. Serve immediately.

Makes 2 dozen

Christians awake!
Salute the happy morn,
Whereon the Saviour
of the world was born!

CHRISTMAS MORNING! WHAT A happy and joyous time. Every family has its own traditions. I will share ours with you.

Even if you awaken earlier, no one is allowed to go downstairs before 7 a.m. When I was young, this was often a very long wait, because Sarah, Ben and I usually woke up much earlier.

At 7 a.m., all three of us would race into our parents' room with happy shouts of "Merry Christmas" and "Get up, get up!" Dad would make a pretence of being too tired and we would have to pull and push him to get him out of bed.

When we all had on slippers and dressing gowns, we would wait at the top of the stairs for Dad to turn on the Christmas tree lights, all the while listening to him saying "Wow!" or "My goodness would you just look at that!" or "Mercy me there is too much here for just one family, I think Santa made a mistake." Finally, he would shout for us to come down and off we would fly.

Usually, one main gift from Santa would be left, unwrapped, under the tree, and we would shriek and clap about our own.

The rule was that we opened our stockings before any other gifts. When the last gift was opened, we would eat our candy canes while mother made breakfast.

Our children and grandchildren continue to follow these rituals, and I can still hear George's voice echoing from the

living room, "My heavens! Look what Santa has brought this
year!"

BREAKFAST ON CHRISTMAS MORNING is usually
substantial as we don't eat again until dinner at around 4
o'clock. One of our favourite breakfasts includes baked apple
pancakes with bacon and sausage. This pancake is both
fabulous and filling.

Baked Apple Pancakes

6 large eggs

1 cup milk

2/3 cup flour

1/2 tsp salt

4 large apples, peeled cored and sliced

4 tbsp lemon juice

5 tbsp butter

1/2 cup brown sugar, lightly packed

1 tsp cinnamon

Dash of nutmeg

Pure maple syrup

Preheat the oven to 400°F. Mix together the eggs, milk, flour
and salt. Toss the apple slices with 2 tbsp lemon juice.

Melt the butter in a 12-inch quiche dish in the oven.
Remove the dish from the oven and lay the apple slices evenly

on the bottom. Return to the oven and bake until the butter sizzles; do not let the apples brown.

Remove from the oven and immediately pour the batter over the apples. Mix together the brown sugar, cinnamon, and nutmeg and sprinkle over the batter.

Bake the pancake for 25–30 minutes. Remove from the oven and slowly drizzle the remaining 2 tsp of lemon juice over the top.

Cut into portions and serve immediately with orange juice, bacon and sausages and you will have a wonderful Christmas breakfast.

Hark! the herald angels sing,
"Glory to the newborn King."

FOR MANY YEARS, GOOSE was the traditional Christmas bird. Although I still enjoy goose, we have come to have turkey for our Christmas dinner almost every year now. My sister, Sarah, passed along her recipe for herb and sausage stuffing and I'm sure you will enjoy it.

Herb and Sausage Stuffing

6 cups stale bread cubes

1 tsp salt

1/2 tsp pepper

2 tbsp chopped parsley

2 tsp dried mixed herbs

1 1/2 tsp poultry seasoning

2 pounds sausage meat

1/4 cup fat (from cooked sausage)

1 cup chopped onion

1 stalk of celery chopped

Combine the bread cubes, salt, pepper, parsley, herbs and poultry seasoning in a large bowl.

Fry the sausage meat gently for about 10 minutes, but do not let the meat brown. Drain the fat, reserving 1/4 cup.

Sauté celery and onions in butter until the onions are transparent (about 7 minutes).

Combine the onions and celery with the seasoned bread cubes. Add the sausage fat then the sausage meat. Add sufficient hot water to hold the stuffing together lightly, but not enough to make a wet mixture.

Roasting the Turkey

Wipe the turkey inside and out with a small cloth wrung out from warm water. Salt the body cavity and the tail end lightly and fill with the stuffing. Do not pack tightly.

Place the turkey on a rack in the roaster. Season the skin with salt and pepper and lay strips of bacon over the breast. Cover the roasting pan with a tent of foil—ensure a tight seal around the pan.

Cooking time is about 20 minutes per pound at 325°F. Remove the foil and the bacon strips for the final half hour to allow the turkey to brown. To test that the bird is cooked, pierce the thick part of the thigh with a fine skewer. The juices should run clear with no trace of pink.

WHAT WOULD A TURKEY dinner be without mashed potatoes. By adding a few extra goodies, you can make your potatoes a special treat. This recipe can be prepared ahead of time, and heated in the microwave at dinner time.

"Do Ahead" Mashed Potatoes

12–14 medium potatoes

1/4 cup butter

1/2 cup milk

8 ounces light cream cheese, softened

16 ounces sour cream

Salt and pepper

Peel the potatoes and cook in boiling water until tender. Remove from heat and drain. Add butter and milk and mash until the potatoes are lump free. Using an electric mixer, blend in the cream cheese and sour cream. Add salt and pepper to taste.

Put the potato mixture in a glass casserole. Cover and refrigerate until needed. Heat in the microwave until completely hot.

Serve with your favourite gravy. If your family loves potatoes, you'd better make lots. These are so good that people will be back for seconds.

WHEN I WAS YOUNG, I used to look forward, all year, to Christmas dinner at Grandma and Grandpa's house. I loved to see all of my cousins and aunts and uncles, but I had two particular favourites. Uncle Bill and Uncle Harry, my mother's two brothers-in-law, were such fun. They each had a tremendous sense of humour and I found everything that they said absolutely hilarious.

Uncle Bill would say something really funny and then Uncle Harry and I would laugh uproariously. Uncle Harry had the most wonderful laugh I have ever heard! It would come roaring up from somewhere near his toes, I think, and just explode out of him. I have seen entire rooms full of people break-up with laughter and have no idea what they were laughing at. That is how terrific Uncle Harry's laugh was.

One Christmas in particular, my dad and my two uncles decided to see who could eat the most. They didn't tell anyone else, but I had overheard them talking in the living room.

"I believe that I'll have more turkey, Mother MacIntosh," said Uncle Bill. "Yes, I will too," said dad and Uncle Harry.

It went on and on. Most of the other children had been excused, but I was anxious to see who would win, so I hung about quietly, so as not to be noticed. "My word! I think I'm going to explode!" said Uncle Harry.

Well, that was too much to see alone, so I raced off to get the others. "Come quick, Uncle Harry's going to explode!" I yelled.

We all raced back to the dining room to wait for the impending combustion. When Uncle Harry found out why we were all staring at him, his laugh came bellowing out of him and we were all a part of the huge joke.

These were wonderful times and cherished memories that have stayed with me for a lifetime.

ALTHOUGH, AS A CHILD, I didn't care very much for turnip, I have come to love this old fashioned vegetable, and I really like it cooked with apple.

Baked Turnip with Apple

6 cups grated yellow turnip

1 large apple, peeled and diced.

2 tbsp light brown sugar

1 tsp salt

1/4 tsp pepper

1/4 cup melted butter or margarine

Mix all ingredients gently but thoroughly, and turn into a buttered 1 1/2 quart casserole. Cover and bake at 350°F for about 1 1/2 hours. Serve hot.

Makes 6 servings

ALTHOUGH THE CHILDREN would have preferred to skip vegetables and get straight to the desserts, we did our best to make an "edible green thing." Sautéed green beans usually interested a few of the children and had the adults raving.

Sautéed Green Beans

1 1/4 pounds green beans
1 tbsp salad oil
1/8 tsp ground black pepper
1 tbsp soy sauce

Trim the ends from the beans and put them in a 3-quart Dutch oven with enough water to cover the beans. Over high heat bring to a boil, then reduce to medium low heat. Simmer 5–10 minutes until the beans are tender crisp, then drain.

In the same Dutch oven, over medium heat, add the salad oil, pepper and soy sauce to the beans and cook, stirring occasionally, until they are tender and begin to brown.

Makes 6 servings

BECAUSE WE HAVE SO many at our Christmas dinner, it's fun to share a wide variety of desserts. Each family makes a dessert to serve 6–8 people. Here are a few of the family's favourites.

Lemon Syllabub

It's a goods thing Christmas comes but once a year; this dessert is sinful.

1 lemon

1/2 cup medium-dry sherry

1/2 cup sugar

2 cups heavy cream or whipping cream

Lemon peel and sprigs of mint for garnish

Grate the peel of the lemon then squeeze out the juice into a large bowl. Add remaining ingredients and beat at medium speed until thick and creamy. Pour into wine glasses and refrigerate at least one hour. Before serving, garnish with lemon peel and mint sprigs if desired.

Makes 10 servings

WE ARE A FAMILY OF pumpkin lovers and pumpkin pie is always a hit. This pumpkin mousse with sugared pecans is just as delectable, but a bit lighter. It goes well at the end of a dinner when you really want pumpkin, but aren't sure if you can eat a piece of pie.

Pumpkin Mousse

1/2 cup pecans, chopped

1 tbsp plus 1/3 cup light brown sugar

1 16-ounce can solid-pack pumpkin (not pumpkin pie mix)

1 package vanilla instant pudding or pie filling (to serve 4)

1 cup milk

1 tsp vanilla extract

3/4 tsp ground cinnamon

1/2 tsp ground ginger

1/2 tsp ground allspice

2 cups heavy cream or whipping cream

In a 2-quart saucepan over medium heat, cook the pecans until they are lightly browned, stirring occasionally. Remove from the heat; stir in 1 tbsp brown sugar until the sugar melts and evenly coats the pecans (about 1 minute). Set aside to cool.

In a large bowl, with a wire whisk, mix pumpkin, pudding mix, milk, vanilla extract, cinnamon, ginger, allspice and remaining brown sugar until well blended.

In a small bowl, with the mixer at medium speed, beat the cream until stiff peaks form. Refrigerate 1 cup of the whipped cream, and fold the rest into the pumpkin mixture.

Spoon the pumpkin mixture into eight 10-ounce goblets, cover and refrigerate until ready to serve. (This dessert tastes best if it has been chilled for at least 1/2 hour before serving.)

To serve, garnish each goblet with whipped cream and sprinkle with sugared pecans.

Serves 8

NO CHRISTMAS, IN OUR family, would be complete without a chocolate dessert and this soufflé cake is a wonderful way
to welcome chocolate into any home.

Chocolate Soufflé Cake

12 tbsp unsalted butter

1 tbsp plus 1/2 cup sugar

3 bars (9 ounces) bittersweet chocolate, in pieces

2 tbsp all-purpose flour

2 tsp vanilla extract

5 large egg yolks

6 large egg whites at room temperature

1/4 tsp cream of tartar

Confectioner's sugar for dusting

Eggnog Sauce:

1 tbsp cornstarch

1 1/2 cups prepared eggnog

Cranberry Coulis:

1 cup cranberries

1/2 cup granulated sugar

1/3 cup water

2 tbsp orange juice

1/2 tbsp orange liqueur or orange juice

Preheat the oven to 350°F. Use 2 tsp of the butter to grease a 9-inch springform pan; with 1 tbsp sugar, coat the sides of the pan only.

In a medium saucepan, melt together the chocolate and the remaining butter over low heat, stirring to blend. Remove saucepan from the heat. Whisk in the remaining sugar, the flour and the vanilla. Cool for 5 minutes. Whisk in yolks, one at a time. Transfer batter to a large bowl and cool completely.

In another large bowl, beat the egg whites until frothy. Add cream of tartar, beat until billowy, firm (but not dry) peaks form. Stir a large spoonful of whites into the chocolate mixture, then, with a rubber spatula, fold in the remaining whites until no white streaks remain.

Pour into the prepared pan and spread evenly. Bake for 35 minutes or until a wooden pick inserted in the centre comes out with moist crumbs attached.

Cool the cake on a rack. (The cake will sink in the middle). Remove pan sides and transfer the cake to a plate. Dust with confectioner's sugar.

To make the sauce: In a small saucepan dissolve the cornstarch in the eggnog and heat to boiling, stirring constantly. Boil 1 minute. Remove from heat. Chill.

To make coulis: In a small saucepan, heat cranberries, sugar and water to boiling. Boil gently 8 minutes or until the cranberries pop. With a rubber spatula press the mixture through a fine mesh sieve placed over a bowl.

To serve: Spoon 3 tbsp of eggnog sauce on each of 8 plates. Top with a slice of cake. Spoon or drizzle some coulis into the sauce. Use a wooden pick to pull the coulis through the sauce to make decorative swirls. This dessert looks as good as it tastes and, believe me, it tastes divine.

CHRISTMAS HAS EVOLVED INTO a celebration of enormous proportions, yet for all of the traditions and customs we come back to the reason for the season, the birth of Jesus Christ nearly 2000 years ago.

May I wish to all of you and your friends and family a very Merry Christmas and, in the words of Tiny Tim, "God Bless us everyone."

Index